NO HUMAN IS ILLEGAL

AN ATTORNEY ON THE FRONT LINES OF THE IMMIGRATION WAR

J. J. Mulligan Sepúlveda

MELVILLE HOUSE
BROOKLYN · LONDON

NO HUMAN IS ILLEGAL

First published in 2018 by Melville House Publishing
Copyright © J. J. Mulligan Sepúlveda, 2018
All rights reserved
First Melville House Printing: January 2019

Melville House Publishing
46 John Street
Brooklyn, NY 11201
and
Suite 2000
16/18 Woodford Road
London E7 0HA

mhpbooks.com
@melvillehouse

ISBN: 978-1-61219-769-2
ISBN: 978-1-61219-770-8 (eBook)

Designed by Betty Lew

Printed in the United States of America
1 3 5 7 9 10 8 6 4 2

A catalog record for this book is available
from the Library of Congress

To my mother,
EMMA,
for passing it on;

To CHLOE and MYA,
for the opportunity to pass it on;

But mostly, of course,
to ALEJANDRA—
tú sabes porqué.

Against the ruin of the world, there is only one defense—the creative act.

—*Kenneth Rexroth*

CONTENTS

INTRODUCTION

Francisco leaned against the wall, his cowboy boots crossed one over the other. We were in a small room with no windows, packed tight with immigrants, two of whom had brought their children. ICE (U.S. Immigration and Customs Enforcement) had ordered Francisco to report to their Enforcement and Removal office that day, and instead of waiting at his house for them to show up anyway during an early-morning raid, he had obliged. In just a few minutes, he would go into custody and thereafter be detained in a detention center nearby, while a team of attorneys rushed to file an appeal for him. He had been in the United States for nineteen years. For the last four years he had been in and out of immigration courtrooms, detained, released on bond, and on this day back into detention, all for a minor offense and a major misunderstanding.

He told me, when we met at the café across the street before walking over, that he had *un pie en la frontera, y uno aqui*, a New Age, immigrant riff on the British axiom "one foot in the grave."

As an immigration lawyer, that is the reality of who we work with and what they experience, a split life—often they are not fully here, but nor are they there. With Donald Trump as president, this experience has expanded such that the question of confinement and deportation now hangs over every immigrant like a guillotine. ICE conducts raids with impunity, un-documented migrants are held in prisonlike detention centers, their fates left in the hands of biased judges and interview officers, and children are being separated from their parents, only to be left orphaned. For the American Dream, the flag flies at half-mast.

Sadly, Trump is only worsening issues ongoing from the Obama administration, which Obama had in turn exacerbated from the Bush administration, and so on. That Trump is possibly the most anti-immigrant president we have ever had does not nullify the country's deeper, systemic issues that Trump has thrived on. To be clear, Donald Trump has not rewritten the immigration laws; he did not create ICE; and he certainly did not invent racism or xenophobia. He is not the first president to ban certain immigrants from entering this country, and he is not the first president to separate families. Whether he is the last to do these things is up to us.

And so while this book is dedicated to immigration lawyers and the work that we do, it is also about our response, as a nation, to these challenges.

I wrote this book because I wanted people to know what it was like to be on the front lines of the immigration war, behind the headlines and at a human level. As the son of a Chilean immigrant who left her country during the Pinochet regime, I empathize with people who want to escape the cruel existences of their native countries for the promising possibilities of an adopted home. This book is for those immigrants who believe the United States could offer them a better life and for those who need to escape one much worse. It depicts many of the journeys that are now required to immigrate, with militarized borders and national policies increasingly hostile to immigrants: across the sea in makeshift rafts, through the desert on foot, aboard a menacing train, hidden in crates, through bombed-out war zones, a thousand sleepless nights in camps. To undertake these perilous journeys, people must be even more desperate to leave than they are hopeful to arrive.

My narrative was formed by experiences that will remain with me for the rest of my life—of cutting my teeth in New York City's immigration court system; of defending immigrants interred at border detention centers; of volunteering at JFK during Trump's travel ban; of traveling to Spain on a Fulbright to study the European refugee crisis; and of helping undocumented teenage boys who are savagely mistreated in California detention facilities. I owe much to my family—my wife, an immigrant to the United States herself, most of all—which has allowed me to pursue this career path that has taken us from coast to coast and to Europe and back. Along the way, I do my best to make immigration law, that bureaucratic morass that adjudicates who is allowed to stay in this country and who is forced to leave, digestible. While the book may be dedicated to immigration lawyers, it is also for everyone to understand the work that we do and the personal and emotional toll it can take, which, while never approximating what our clients suffer, is nonetheless intertwined and often inseparable. Indeed, this book began entirely as a therapeutic exercise in coping with vicarious trauma; to be able to tell this story as well as protect my sources, I have obscured the identities of some of my clients.

This book, like our jobs as immigration lawyers, lies at the intersection of the legal system and immigrant lives. It comes at a time when who we say we are as a country and what we do to the people who most need America and its Dream is in jeopardy. It is also but one story among the countless of those who have made it their mission to help others live their lives in this country, many of whom are themselves immigrants or first generation. Without humanity, laws are just words that set out minimum standards. Without humanity, the United States can no longer carry the torch of the free world. This book is for those who refuse to let that flame die.

NO HUMAN
IS ILLEGAL

PART I

THE WORK

. . . .

"I don't consider myself a real lawyer. I'm not
a lawyer in the sense that the better job I do,
the more money I get from my client. I'm just
trying to help . . . You can change a few things.
But not much progress is being made. There are
about two thousand of us in the country. The
legislatures are not controlled by us. For every
law we have declared unconstitutional, they
write five more. For every step we make, we're
pushed back four. Some days I'm optimistic.
Other days . . ."

—*Philip da Vinci, from Studs Terkel's* Working

It began with an intake.

This was where I would interview immigrant youth seeking relief from deportation and looking to be put on a path toward lawful status. The intake was only the initial meeting, but like being at an interview for a life-changing job, the immigrant youth would often be nervous, scared, shy, or uncertain. They believed that there were right answers to the questions I asked. And they were not wrong: certain answers would qualify them for relief, while others would not. Because I needed to be able to back up their information, it didn't serve them to lie to me or to change the facts or circumstances of their lives, and therefore their answers needed to be answered truthfully. That, I would assure them, was the only right answer.

The questions were simple at the start—*Where were you born? When were you born?*—and became more specific as the intake went on. What resulted was a composite of a person's life, rendered as a list of clues that helped assess the person's eligibility for relief. Asking the right questions was like trying to find the right turns that would lead one out of a labyrinth. I would take a few steps down one corridor of inquiry—asking some question designed to gauge eligibility for asylum—to see if that route was viable, and if not, I would pursue another path. The better you knew what qualified for relief, the more options you had for making a defense: family-based sponsorship, prosecutorial discretion, DACA (Deferred Action for Childhood Arrivals), the full-range of humanitarian relief, acquisition or derivation of citizenship, even a quick peek down employment sponsorship. Sometimes, the most inane question could lead toward an unexpected solution to legally keep the youth from being deported.

Because I came to know what kinds of cases were eligible, I would sometimes get a nauseating hope during an intake, contradictory to every humane impulse that led me to this work in the first place. I *wanted* something bad to have happened to the immigrant youth I was interviewing, something that would have allowed me to help them win their case. Sex trafficking or sexual assault could lead to a T visa or a U visa, but even that wasn't guaranteed. The entire process, with all its loopholes, restrictions, prejudices, and bureaucracy, was like being enveloped in a sociopolitical satire—Paul Beatty for immigrants—yet it was anything but funny. The immigrant youth who were not eligible for relief haunted my mind for days. I second-guessed myself, I'd review the facts two, three, four times. I'd toy with ethical violations. Could I have bent the truth a little? The truth is moldable, isn't it? We learn in law school that truths are moldable; that is a basic pillar of a legal education. These were the lost cases, where I would constantly be looking for loopholes, for missed details, for unseen possibilities. It's only when I searched to exhaustion that I made myself let it go.

If the intake was my first meeting with an immigrant youth, it could be hard for the person to talk about his or her past trauma. No matter how much they wanted a lawyer to represent them in their immigration case, it might be difficult for immigrant youths to trust me. For instance, it could be challenging for women to share stories about rape or sexual abuse, particularly if the incident was recent and she was reluctant to be behind closed doors with a man. Conversely, for young men, especially from Central America, sharing their feelings about certain things in their life might go against their ingrained *machismo*. Many Central American youth unable to reunite with parents due to abuse or neglect often qualified for Special Immigrant Juvenile Status (SIJS). Though this would have allowed them to stay in the United States as a lawful resident, many youths were reluctant to talk about parental violence, replying *No era mucho* or *No me acuerdo* to minimize the events. This is where the right questions and trust would become key. Instead of *Would your parents ever beat you?* I would try and work up to it. *Would your parents ever get upset with you? If you did something they thought was wrong, what would happen?* Many youths still missed their parents, despite the mistreatment they faced, because they had no one else and because child/parent relationships are complicated in every part of the world, especially in countries where physical discipline is still the norm.

Intakes were among my earliest experiences as an immigration lawyer, back when I worked for Atlas: DIY, an organization that provided free legal services for undocumented immigrant youth. I would learn that most of the immigrant youth we worked with had just arrived in this country, alone, and someone somewhere told them they could find free lawyers here. Because our organization would present seminars on immigration relief at local high schools, a counselor or principal would send a young person to us, thinking that maybe the youth could qualify for immigration relief. Other times they might have heard about us at a church or library, where we would provide Know-Your-Rights training sessions. Or they heard about us through word of mouth from a former client who claimed that we had provided him or her with a green card. What they didn't tell them is just how difficult it is to be eligible for one. If, after we conducted an intake, the person turned out to be ineligible for immigration relief, there could be confusion and vocalized resentment. What mattered was that they found their way to our office, and we would try to help as best we could.

Some immigrant youths would discover our organization at immigration court, where our organization's name, address, and phone number appeared on preprinted, alphabetized sheets provided by the legal services department, which is supposed to hand out such documents to all Unaccompanied Alien Children (so-called UACs). These were the youths who appeared before an immigration judge on the "rocket docket," cases that are given rapid-fire hearings. The UACs were under eighteen and had arrived in the United States alone, which triggered this designation and was supposed to grant them certain special protections under immigration law.

On my first day, a Monday, I arrived to find the doors still locked. While Millie, the deputy director, and I had shown up on time, no one else had. We had coffee downstairs and got to know each other until Leslie, the executive director, hair still wet from the shower, rushed past us, coffee in one hand, phone to ear in the other. She was a human tornado of spirit often seen in activists: fearless and stubborn, galvanized by her perpetual grudge against the status quo. She had founded Atlas: DIY with three young immigrant women who had been former clients of hers at another organization. Until Atlas became the recipient of grant funding and fellowships, these four women had made up the entire company.

Leslie was still a lawyer, but only nominally practicing. She still had cases dating back to the time of the organization's founding a few years prior that needed to be closed or appealed, and these she handed off to me during my first two days, with rapid explanations before rushing on to the next thing. She was always busy, even when she wasn't. Leslie also kept picking up cases from random people she'd meet—taxi drivers, bodega clerks, even a friend's housekeeper. She said she wasn't practicing anymore—and it was an open question as to whether her bar license was still active—but she couldn't help herself. She couldn't say no. It didn't help that on the day I had arrived, Becky, the lead attorney on our legal team, was in court all day and would be out of the office the following week. I had been assigned her cases, which gave me only four days to learn everything I needed to know to keep Becky's open cases moving along smoothly. Nor did it help that I was a fresh-faced lawyer who had just taken the New York State bar exam a few weeks prior.

Which meant that my experience was minimal when I met Elvis, one of my earliest intakes and the first immigrant youth I would represent in removal proceedings. Elvis was a sweet, polite kid who addressed me formally as *licensiado*, or "attorney," in the same way people would address a cop as "officer." He had come to us of his own volition.

Though Elvis was shy in the first few minutes of our intake, as we eased into the questioning, his answers began to flow more easily and became lengthier. But even as he divulged his story and circumstances, I needed to sift through them for the right kind of information. Entire lives could be squeezed onto one or two sheets of paper from a yellow legal pad. The questions asked—tried, practiced, and given to desired results— were not specific to each youth, at least initially. Instead they began templated and became personalized as the intake proceeded. None were perfect word-for-word matches for the immigration law statutes that provided for immigration relief, which is why my job required constantly finessing square pegs into ever-shrinking round holes. This was very much what happened with Elvis as I jotted down notes during his intake, taking various tunnels until I came upon what I hoped would be the most plausible case for him to receive relief.

Intake with Elvis, 8/18/15

- *DOB: 17 y.o. (06/12/1998)*
- *Country: El Salvador*
- *No relationship with biological father; mother recently deceased, not gang-related*
- *9 siblings, none USCs—five here in U.S.*
  - *Only one sibling is not half-sibling—she's in El Salvador, but coming soon according to Elvis*
- *Lives w/ five half-brothers, all undoc.*
  - *One brother accidentally shot 8 years ago, not gang-related*
- *Has not spoken to father in 10+ years*
  - *Doesn't know where he is*
  - *Waiver of service needed, or last known address*
- *Arrived in 2013, three weeks in detention*
  - *Brother here in BK=sponsor*
  - *Not priority (PD?)*
- *In removal proceedings*
  - *Next court date Jan. 2016*
  - *Has had two MC hearings already*

· *Minimal contact w/ gangs*
  ◦ *No other asylum issues*

· *No contact w/ police in U.S.*
  ◦ *No U visa issues*

· *Came to U.S. for better life and to work and be with brothers*
  ◦ *Works and goes to school—No T visa issues*

· *SIJS best avenue so far*

· *In school*
  ◦ *Need school records*

· *Has moved since arriving in NYC*
  ◦ *No longer at address listed in his files*
  ◦ *Update address at next hearing*

When we finished speaking that day, I told Elvis that I could represent him, if he wanted, in his immigration proceedings. "*Gracias, licensiado,*" he said, then asked quietly how much I would charge him. When I said that there would be no charge, he repeated, a bit softer this time, "*Gracias, licensiado,*" then looked away, out the window. I explained the basics of Special Immigrant Juvenile Status and outlined a plan for the upcoming months before his next immigration court hearing in January: have a follow-up meeting, prepare documents and motions, get paperwork from El Salvador, meet with his brother, file in family court, and so on. I tried to sound confident, listing the steps as if I had done this a thousand times before. Elvis didn't notice. He just needed a lawyer.

———

The United States Code has the following to say about the Right to Counsel in immigration proceedings:

> *In any removal proceedings before an immigration judge and in any appeal proceedings before the Attorney General from any such removal proceedings, the person concerned shall have the privilege of being represented (at no expense to the Government) by such counsel, authorized to practice in such proceedings, as he shall choose.*

The words in parentheses are key. Rather than a tangent to overlook, they hollow out the sentence, render almost every other word superfluous. Immigrants have the privilege of representation, but *at no expense to the government.* A similar sentiment is found in the U.S. healthcare system: anyone has the privilege of being attended by a doctor, but the government will not pay for it. The "privilege" of representation that is spoken of in the U.S. Code in fact often precludes representation for immigrants because "at no expense to the Government" means at full expense to the immigrant. In practical terms, this might especially mean no representation for immigrant youth. Nonprofits, if they exist in the area where the immigrant lives, are often inundated with pending cases and unable to take on new ones. Private attorneys could cost thousands of dollars.

Contrast this with criminal proceedings, where thanks to the famous *Gideon v. Wainright* case, everyone is provided counsel—a public defender—even if they can't afford it. This means that a person who plants a bomb in a park, for example, is given counsel when they are tried for the crime if they cannot afford it, but a fifteen-year-old immigrant being deported back to a war-torn nation is not. The difference, according to the Supreme Court, is that deportation is not a "punishment" that would warrant such constitutional protections as going to jail would. Imagine having to tell that to a teenage immigrant who had fled the danger of gangs, who must defend himself in front of an immigration judge, and from a veteran Department of Homeland Security (DHS) attorney. It would be a laughable scenario, one that would seem implausible, like a Little Leaguer going up against a Yankees pitcher—and yet, it has occurred often. It has even occurred with much younger immigrants. Recently, in the summer of 2018, a one-year-old went in front of an immigration judge alone. It is very difficult to represent yourself if you don't know immigration law at all; it is impossible if you are still using a pacifier.

To get counsel and have a semblance of a fair fight, immigrant youths need to find a lawyer, either a free one or one who doesn't charge exorbitant fees, while in a new city and country and barely speaking the language. It is hard enough making friends in their new high school, but an immigrant youth is likely also worried about paying off a debt to a *coyote*; not paying off such a debt can be devastating for family members back home, who may be dismembered, raped, kidnapped, or perpetually threatened for debt repayment purposes. Many family members have put up their land as collateral and have accepted interest rates of 15–20 percent; as Lauren Markham depicted in her book *The Far Away Brothers*, that land is often their only possession of value and working it their livelihood.

Private immigration lawyers and *notarios*—often immigrants already here for an extended period of time who have figured out how to scheme the newest arrivals into massive fees for work they are not lawfully allowed to do—are willing and able to charge almost any amount they want. Ours was a client population that had little to no understanding of the legal process they were being subjected to or what competence looked like. They would meet with a private attorney or *notario* and leave the case in his or her hands, which was exactly what the attorney or *notario* wanted and encouraged them to do. *I'll take care of everything*, wronged clients would tell me their previous lawyers had told them. Famous last words for anyone working with a lawyer, but more so in immigration law. Immigration cases can take years to resolve, so immigrants often did not know when they had been taken advantage of or when their case had been mishandled. By then, it was too late.

There were cultural norms and beliefs that came into play during an intake as well, namely that something free must be broken, a scam, or generally not as good as something you paid for. Many immigrants I spoke with were skeptical that I was a free lawyer and were constantly asking me, *What's the catch?* Or they thought they would get better representation from me or Becky if they offered us money. One client went so far as to sneak four hundred dollars into a thank-you card; I had to chase the person down the block to give it back. Ironically, the opposite, in terms of the private-immigration-law bar, was true in the United States, with a few exceptions. Numerous judges on the federal bench and in immigration court had stated the gross inadequacy of nearly half the private immigration attorneys that appeared before them. Immigration law could be the last stop for lawyers who had not been able to make it anywhere else, for many of the reasons already stated previously: naive client population, the possibility of high fees, and little-to-no repercussions for incompetence because there were always more clients. In the United States, immigration was big business, but it wasn't a fair one.

One of the proponents who addressed the problem of inadequate representation and access to justice was none other than a circuit court judge. Robert A. Katzmann, Chief Judge of the U.S. Court of Appeals for the Second Circuit, was dismayed with the lack of representation in immigration proceedings. He commissioned a study that found immigrants were six times more likely to be successful in their cases if they had counsel. Judge Katzmann conceived of a fellowship in which immigration lawyers would be given salary-equivalent grants to work at various immigration nonprofits around the Northeast and beyond. In 2013, with the help of the Robin Hood Foundation, the Immigration Justice Corps Fellowship was born. Two years later, the second class of twenty-five fellows were announced, myself included, with each of us being assigned to different immigration advocacy nonprofits across New York.

It wasn't only newbie immigration attorneys who were jump-started by grant money; nonprofits were buoyed by new grant money as well. Until it had received two multinational grants, Atlas: DIY could be found under an eight-lane overpass in a cramped two-room office that shook with the traffic. I arrived only a couple of weeks after it had moved into a riverside office in Sunset Park, soon enough to hear stories of computer screens shaking during heavy traffic and intakes being conducted with limited privacy. Because it was a new organization, Atlas: DIY had struggled to get funding until the time I went to work for them. The new office, unlike the one faced by the veteran staff, was big enough for the brand-new legal team to have its own suite, complete with private spaces to conduct intakes.

Our new office, in reality, was two large apartments separated by a hallway between them. We reformed and improvised this into one office, but with different spaces for different programs: our college-access program and other nonlegal programming on one side of the hall and the legal suite on the other side of the hall, where, for confidentiality purposes, you could only enter accompanied by a legal-staff member. Our part-time social worker also had a small space that doubled as the makeshift library, where she conducted counseling sessions twice a week, across from one of the bathrooms.

We kept the office supplies on the legal side in the kitchen, with our legal library—a generous term that we mostly used ironically for our eleven books—in the cupboard above the sink, next to the sugar, instant coffee, tea, and mugs. I opened our copy of the Immigration and Nationality Act once and a dead roach fell onto my desk. Ants, searching for sugar, would often form a black line, marching along the bindings of the thick legal treatises. We didn't need much of a legal library because most things we could find online. The problem was that those websites, like Westlaw or LexisNexis, which provided all of the case law possible, were paid services that we could not afford. We found a way in: the websites offered free unlimited use to law students to hopefully entice them to use their services after law school. When we had legal interns, we copied down their log-in information and used these for our legal research. It was a win-win: the more legal research you did, the more points you accumulated with Westlaw or LexisNexis, which you could turn in for prizes as small as a coffee mug and as large as a flat-screen television. Our legal interns nearly always had enough for the biggest prizes.

If we had a party or celebration, it was held not in the suite, where the legal team worked, but in what we called "Casa," a safe space for immigrant youth that were pursued by ICE and responsibilities and traumatic memories. Casa had couches, tables, board games, and a refrigerator and pantry with food. We did our best to get healthy food for the young immigrants, but most of them wanted Cup O' Noodles, peanut butter and jelly sandwiches, and chips and salsa, and we obliged. When we would buy organic oat bars, they were always the last to go, eaten only when absolutely nothing else remained. Casa was where the immigrant youth came to hang out after school, after work, or during summer when they had nowhere else to be. We had sleepovers there before early-morning trips to protest sites and offered the space to families who were scared to go home because ICE had come looking for them and would be coming back. Casa faced the programming side and was separated from the rest of the office by a half wall, and when privacy was needed, a blue curtain could be used to make a full wall. Our deputy director, director of outreach, and director of operations in their cubicles would always hear the chewing, talking, and laughter from Casa. They would put music on to drown out the noise and unconsciously, those in Casa would talk or laugh louder. Each side would escalate the volume until finally headphones would be used, and then it would be difficult to call anyone on the programming side.

Our guiding philosophy was to empower the immigrant youth and evolve our process so that they become "members" and "leaders" of the organization. They decided their activities; they guided the organization. As the organization was for them, it was in their hands—for the most part. In practice, it did not always work as beautifully as it sounds, but the idea is important: immigrant youth, forever being told who will be saving them, were given a voice in their cases and their fate. As attorneys, we would partner with them and keep them fully aware of what was happening. And when this occurred, and young people got to know the intricacies of how the law affected their cases as well as the impact it had on immigrants in our society, they would take this knowledge back to the communities, which would in turn spread the empowerment.

Casa was also where I led a men's support group on Monday

nights. In its inception, it had high aspirations beginning with the name we gave the meetings, but it devolved into a hangout session with me and eight to ten immigrant youths from Central America eating pizza and talking. We had no set schedule or outline for those Monday nights. We went where it took us. We had a twenty-dollar budget and would often order two pizzas. Once, we saved up for five weeks, eating only the chips and salsa always available in Casa while we talked. We took the hundred dollars and went to a pool hall, where we rented three tables and played for hours together. Some in the group had never played pool and needed to be shown how to shoot. Others were regular sharks and beat me handily. I thought of Paul Newman as Fast Eddie Felson as we played, a reference no one understood when I shared it with those at the same table as me, though many would likely relate to the character's down-and-out hunger to make it.

Sometimes there would be little children in Casa painting or drawing on the walls, while their young mothers and fathers were across the hall meeting with someone from the legal team. From his desk, our front desk manager would keep an eye on the kids. Toys were scattered around the floor. Markers and paper were laid out on tables. Sometimes paint too. Traces of these visitors, in blue, orange, red, and green remained on the tables and walls. Diapers were often changed right on the office couches, including my daughter Chloe's, when I took her to work.

The best part about the office, though, was the people. On any given day, the full-time staff members would be augmented by another five or so volunteers and interns, two part-time staff members, and upwards of twenty people stopping by for a visit, an appointment, or to get information about our organization. The staff alone came from places as diverse as Puerto Rico, Vietnam, and New Jersey, both immigrants and descendants. Some on our staff had their own immigration cases pending. Spanish and Mandarin and Cantonese and French Creole, among other languages, floated across the rooms, came through the phones, and was plastered on our walls. Every sign we put up was at least trilingual. Above the front desk, in the waiting area just outside of Casa, the first thing that most people noticed was a large map with pins and string radiating out from New York and connecting to dozens and dozens of places around the world—a web of solidarity that represented where the immigrant youth came from. We wanted it to feel welcoming even if there were days when it was loud and hectic, as it was on the day Elvis first came into our office. He was so shy that, had someone not spotted him sitting in a corner, he might have been altogether missed.

Elvis, who had not had a safe place to live in El Salvador and whose apartment in Bay Ridge was crowded to overflowing, soon found a second home in our offices, where he could do his homework and get help in English, borrow Spanish-language books, or be alone on a couch with his headphones in and his eyes resting. He learned to speak louder on some days, and on other days his presence seemed to make things quieter. He made friends and gradually grew into his new life in the United States. For an undocumented immigrant in this country, however, what we offered in Casa was a salve, not a solution. The ultimate win of lawful status lay in the hands of immigration judges and officials.

———

New York City's primary immigration court was located near Manhattan's City Hall at 26 Federal Plaza. Most people familiar with the court simply called it "26 Fed." The FBI had an office in the building, which was why, upon entering the marble foyer, a consistently updated "10 Most Wanted" list greeted visitors, complete with photos and detailed descriptions of their crimes. It seemed like a simple coincidence, but on my first visit, I took it as further proof of the intersection of civil and criminal matters—or, the criminalization of immigration. The building itself was forty-one stories tall, the tallest federal building in the country, and had an almost Soviet-style aesthetic. Alternating black and khaki squares were interposed with windows along its eastern side. Only its western side, constructed at a later date, was slightly more modern.

It was with Elvis that I made my first appearance at 26 Fed, and on that morning, I met him in the front of the building's glass doors, the very same entrance where I had watched Sandra Bullock ask for Ryan Reynolds's hand in marriage in *The Proposal*. Unlike the film, attending immigration court or a USCIS (U.S. Citizenship and Immigration Services) interview here had as much glamour as going through airport security, with your hearing notice serving as a boarding pass: shoes, belt, jacket(s) off, everything out of your pockets and into the trays, bags through the x-ray machine and you through the metal detector. Thankfully, no one would be passed through the massive full-body scanners that populate most American airports today.

Elvis was nervous as we passed through security and into the marble foyer, where a smiling President Obama and Vice President Biden hung on the walls. Theirs were designed to be welcoming smiles, but there was a different truth hidden behind the gesture, one which Elvis and others knew quite well. Elvis and I tried to decipher the elevators together, as certain elevators only went to certain floors and some floors were completely off-limits. The immigration courtrooms were located on either the twelfth or fourteenth floor, but if you went to the twelfth floor and later must go to the fourteenth floor, you had to go back down and switch elevators. Of course, on this first visit, Elvis and I got off on the twelfth floor and then discovered—after reading a large printout of all the days' cases, alphabetized by the last name of the immigrant, posted near the filing window on the twelfth floor—that we needed to be on the fourteenth floor. I felt uneasy with Elvis next to me, looking for his name among a lengthy black-and-white list; it could be difficult to imagine, but these hundred or so names were all on the government's list for removal—and those were just that day's cases.

Most immigrants had their court-appearance information mailed to them, but Elvis had moved, and he and his ORR (Office of Refugee Resettlement) sponsor—his half brother—did not know that they needed to update the court, meaning that none of the mail Elvis was supposed to receive came to him. Things like this happened quite often. That was why it was not unheard of for immigrants to be ordered removed *in absentia* for a variety of reasons such as a change in address, stolen mail, or in the case of a person I represented, one date mistaken for another because some clerk penned a May 1 that looked too much like a May 7. Many immigrants wouldn't even know they had a final order of removal until they met with an attorney who called the Executive Office for Immigration Review (EOIR), which provided an automated hotline for the immigration court system. Once their alien registration number, or A-number, a unique nine-digit number assigned to most immigrants, was entered, the automated system would say: "This person was ordered removed on May 1, 2016 in front of Judge . . . at 26 Federal Plaza." Then, the attorney must break the news and strategize how to reopen the case and get the removal order rescinded—a task that got more difficult after the statutory time limit had elapsed, which it often did.

I had called the EOIR hotline the day before and entered Elvis's A-number. The A-number functions as a sort of social security number for immigrants, though it offers little benefit other than the Department of Homeland Security knowing who you are, which isn't really a benefit at all. Through the hotline, I found out the date and time of the hearing, but through sheer nervousness, I made my first in a series of errors by neglecting to write down the name of the judge. If I had known that it would be Judge Cheng, who was at that time the head judge of the New York Immigration Court, I would have been even more nervous.

Before September 11, immigration courts and the enforcement side of immigration were housed in the Immigration and Naturalization Service (INS). This meant that government prosecutors and border patrol officials worked in the same agency, and were thus colleagues, with the judges who ruled on removal cases they had begun or were prosecuting. In 2002, in response to the attacks of 9/11, where the terrorists had entered the United States with student and visitor visas, DHS was created with broad powers to detain and deport immigrants and collect massive amounts of data in order to protect the United States from the threat of terrorists. It replaced the INS, and subsequently the immigration courts were moved to the Department of Justice. This put the attorney general in charge of the immigration courts, which included the Executive Office for Immigration Review and the Board of Immigration Appeals (BIA). Despite not being specifically named or described in the immigration law statute, the BIA issued precedent-setting decisions deciding, for example, if certain groups of individuals could be eligible for asylum. But even those decisions could be overturned by the attorney general if he or she disagreed with them, a power that would be greatly taken advantage of during the tenure of Jeff Sessions.

The immigration courts thus became separate from the

agency tasked with enforcing the immigration laws after the creation of DHS, the newly created Immigration and Customs Enforcement (ICE), which became one of the three new immigration agencies under the DHS umbrella, along with United States Citizenship and Immigration Services (USCIS) and Customs and Border Protection (CBP). The newly created DHS had the direct effect of weaponizing the immigration laws of the United States, which had seen a severe tightening with the passage of the Illegal Immigration Reform and Immigrant Responsibility Act of 1996 and with the supposedly looming threat of future terrorist attacks. The immigration courts were quickly overwhelmed and have never recovered. The legal process, however minimal, afforded to every immigrant could not and still cannot keep up with the ruthless efficiency of immigration raids.

With the militarization of the border, including the construction of seven hundred additional miles of border wall following the passage of the Secure Fence Act of 2006, and the advent of border detention centers, immigration hearings began to take place along the border in an "anything goes" setting for immigrants and their lawyers. In those hearings, due process of law was often all of two minutes long. And the aftermath was equally as swift. If an undocumented Mexican national had a morning hearing and lost, that person could end up on the Mexican side of the border before lunchtime. At immigration courts in cities like New York, cases were much more nuanced and spaced out, sometimes excruciatingly so. I had had clients who received hearing notices in 2016 for a court date in 2019.

Courts like these were where the backlog of cases was felt most. Here an immigrant's case could either be assigned to an individual or a master calendar hearing. Individual hearings were what they sound like, two attorneys—the government's prosecuting attorney from ICE and an immigration attorney like myself—presenting arguments before a judge as to why this person should be removed or why the person qualified for a certain form of immigration relief. There were also some *pro se* versions of these hearings without an immigration lawyer to represent the immigrants. The individual hearings were conducted in an otherwise empty courtroom, since many traumatic and personal things would be laid out and debated. Stories of being violently raped, of seeing loved ones murdered before their eyes, of being threatened with death and dismemberment if they return to their country, were so common that immigration lawyers and the judge hardly flinched. Some judges took their roles to mean that they could not show compassion because it was too close to gullibility. And so they grilled each immigrant on their traumas like a suspicious boss whose employee wanted to call in sick.

A master calendar hearing, in contrast, was devoid of intimacy. Rather it was more like a cattle call—a judge would go through the bare bones of thirty to forty cases in a single morning sitting. While an immigration judge in many cases would not have the ultimate authority to decide on who was eligible for certain forms of immigration relief—that job often fell to the United States Citizenship and Immigration Services—he or she could make decisions that would greatly impact what would happen to an immigrant: push the case out for another master calendar hearing at a later date; set the case for an individual hearing; order the immigrant removed *in absentia* if the person did not show up for the hearing; or perhaps terminate or administratively close the proceedings. Because the applications were filed with USCIS and they decided whether to approve or deny the immigration relief sought, an immigration judge would often terminate or administratively close removal proceedings while USCIS decided on the application. This was like shutting a book: you were not technically reading, but the book would still be on your nightstand, ready to be reopened. It could take a significant amount of time for USCIS to decide on an application for relief, and immigration judges usually preferred not to have the case on their already bloated docket while they waited. The immigrant, on the other hand, would be left in an extended holding pattern, like applying to a dream university and waiting years to know if you were accepted.

If this all sounds tedious, confusing, and even cruel, that's because it is. The immigration courts are backlogged, disorganized, and often merciless. This was true during the Obama administration, and it is especially true now with the exponential increase in removal proceedings, the constantly receding respect for the rule of law, and the lack of empathy that has characterized the Trump administration. As time went on, some cases that might have had a shot before were doomed. And it would only get worse.

No diagram or schooling could fully prepare an attorney for immigration court. We learned from the nuances of each case, by training to prepare for various and unexpected scenarios, and by paying attention to what drew out the sympathies and scorn of court officials, but overwhelmingly, we learned by doing. This meant being a zealous advocate, as the Model Rules of Professional Conduct for our profession stated, though in ways that the Model Rules could never imagine, given the surprises we faced at every step of the way in immigration cases and with the current administration.

Judge Cheng was the first judge I would go before as an immigration lawyer, and I swiftly learned a few things. She was a veteran of the INS, and though she had a reputation for fairness, she still cut an intimidating figure. When I arrived in the courtroom that October day with Elvis, she was perched on the bench, her black hair cut into shoulder-length strands with straight bangs coming down to the middle of her forehead, blending into her judicial robe to create a black square frame from which her face looked out onto her courtroom. She spoke low and fast, while maintaining an incredulous countenance.

Upon arriving to court, the first thing an immigration lawyer was supposed to do was register with the clerk who sat adjacent to the judge, the judge's right-hand man or woman without whom the courtroom would not function. The clerk was tasked with deposing the attorney's client's file in a horizontal file holder leafed with similar cases, while noting absentees. Throughout the rapid-fire master calendar hearing, the judge would then remove file after file from this stack, each time calling out the last three digits in an immigrant's A-number. This was the first thing I observed, and I made a mental note to keep Elvis's number close at hand.

While that might have been wise, my next move was not. Separating the counsel's table from the clerk and judge was a wooden gate that I knew I had to enter in order to check in. The gate was a holdover from another time, and its formalities of how and when to enter it were learned in the courtroom rather than a classroom. As a law student, I had watched as attorneys cavalierly opened the wooden gate to approach the clerk, even when there was an ongoing hearing for another case. Having seen this and assuming it was common practice, I saw no reason to wait for the hearing to be over and I opened the wooden gate to approach the clerk. And then I heard a raised voice that stopped me in my tracks. It was coming from Judge Cheng, who had inched closer to the microphone and was no longer focusing on the case before her. Instead her eyes were trained on me.

"Counsel, what do you think you're doing?" She was addressing me during an open hearing, which meant that everything she said was being recorded. Behind her words I could feel her face rendering unsaid thoughts: *You fucking idiot.*

"Uh, just going . . . I was going to check in, Your Honor."

My voice cracked like a teenager. Behind me was a packed gallery, where attorneys and their clients filled the benches. On the other side of the wooden gate, the prosecuting ICE attorney and the respondent's attorney turned to look at me, as did the immigrant he was representing, a young woman of about twenty-five with bright eyes and slumping shoulders. Even the court interpreter had turned to stare at me. I was sweating.

"No. You wait there at the gate. My clerk will come to you when she is ready to check you in." Or, as her face told me: *Don't ever fucking try that again.*

"Right. Sorry, Your Honor."

I closed the gate. Though Judge Cheng continued with the hearing, I could still feel everyone's eyes upon me. I didn't know what to do. There were no seats left, so I had to decide whether to keep standing there, every inch of my sweating six-foot-six frame blocking the view of half the courtroom, or beat a retreat to just outside the courtroom entrance, with my head peering in through the open door. If I did that, however, I worried that the clerk wouldn't come retrieve me and we would never be checked in. If that happened, would Elvis be ordered removed *in absentia*? So I just stood there avoiding everyone's glances, questions swirling in my mind, for what seemed like much too long. Mercifully, Elvis was waiting outside for me to call him in and did not witness what had transpired. Before I could decide what to do, the clerk, who had finished whatever she was doing on her computer, at last came over to check me in.

"Last three of the A-number?" she asked.

"Eight Seven Three."

"You got an E-28 on file already?"

My eyes widened. Shit. She was referring to the Notice of Entry of Appearance. Both the judge and the ICE attorney needed to know my information and that I was representing Elvis. This was done by filling out two copies of form E-28, which *must* be on green-hued paper. I had not done this.

"I'm sorry, I—"

The clerk cut me off and pointed to a stack of blank E-28s hanging from a metal magazine rack to the right of us, just reachable from beyond the wooden gate. They seemed to gently bob in the arctic air-conditioning of the courtroom. I had to squeeze past five people sitting in the front row of the benches in the gallery to get to them.

"Where do I fill these out?"

She shrugged. "Some people sit on the floor outside the courtroom."

I took two copies and exited the room. Elvis was leaning in the corridor opposite the doors and I gave him an awkward thumbs up. In that moment, my shirt was entirely sweated through and I was scared that it had begun seeping out to my suit jacket. I may have been a nervous wreck, but I didn't want Elvis to know that.

At the time, I did not know that my status as a pro bono attorney would have made things easier. For instance, if you informed the clerk that you worked at a nonprofit organization or otherwise were doing your work free of charge, you got moved to the front of the line and your case was the first to be called. This was ideal because a judge without fatigue was more likely to be considerate and an attorney who had not had to wait around for three hours in a Wi-Fi-less stupor was more likely to be prepared. The pro bono line-cutting was an unwritten rule that saved the attorney the hassle of waiting in the competitive check-in line that tended to form outside an immigration courtroom before its doors had been unlocked, since cases were called in the order that the attorneys arrived. Our legal system also favored those who obtained counsel—unrepresented immigrants who must represent themselves, *pro se,* in immigration court were made to go last. Because I had yet to learn all the tricks of the trade, I didn't notify the clerk of my pro bono status, and we didn't get to cut in line that day. Instead, Elvis would be the last case called before the unrepresented immigrant cases would be heard, and that wouldn't be for several hours.

The time did not pass quickly, it never did when anticipation was unbearable. We eventually found seats in the gallery after the first hour when several attorneys and their clients finished their cases. Still, I listened intently to as much of the twenty or so cases in front of us as I could, using what was said to formulate a concrete plan of action. One standard tactic that immigration attorneys usually deploy was to decline to give a country of designation for removal. This was primarily symbolic, since the ICE attorney answered the question immediately after, but the gesture was a small resistance, like saying *My client will not be deported, so why would I agree on a country to deport him to?* Or that's how I saw it, at least. As I watched the remaining cases go up before Judge Cheng, I began to recite in my head *I respectfully decline to designate a country of removal.*

When Judge Cheng finally yelled out 8-7-3, the digits correctly lining up with those written on Elvis's maroon file in my hands, my mind went blank. I cautiously opened the wooden gate, some part of me expecting to be stopped again, and Elvis and I made our way to the respondent's table to our right. Though I speak Spanish, Elvis was given a court-appointed interpreter who sat on his other side. Whether it was stage fright or a recollection of my earlier blunder, I once again felt myself going nervous with sweat. A finger tapped me on my shoulder and I turned to find the ICE attorney requesting the copy of the E-28 I was supposed to give her before I sat down. Then I heard the click of a button and turned to Judge Cheng speaking "on the record" into the recorder. She launched into an introduction, the same one, word-for-word, that I would hear her recite at subsequent trials and which I had just heard two dozen times: "This is Judge Cheng in New York City Immigration Court on October 29, 2015 in the removal proceedings of Elvis—A-number two-zero-eight-four-four-five-eight-seven-three . . ." and so on until she asked for my name. For some reason, rather than stating my legal name, the one I wrote on the E-28 now in Judge Cheng's hands, I gave my nickname instead.

"That's not the name I have here," she said.

I corrected myself and for the second time that day could feel the audience in the gallery staring at me. While I stewed in self-consciousness, Judge Cheng asked a question that took a moment for me to realize had been directed at me. Without registering what she had asked me, I panicked and started with the rote memorization I had done.

"Your Honor, we admit allegations one through four and concede removability and we *respectfully* decline—"

"Counsel, listen to my question please," Judge Cheng interrupted before I could embarrass myself further. "Is Respondent still living at the same address?" She read off the address where Elvis used to live with his ORR sponsor. Her look was beyond incredulous; her eyebrows alone seemed to say *Did he really just say that?*

"Ah, no, Your Honor."

"Then you need to fill out an EOIR-33 for change of address. There are copies on the table in front of you. What is his new address, counsel?"

The interpreter was chuckling through his interpretation of what just happened. Elvis looked confused. I confirmed with Elvis that the address I had handwritten on a piece of paper was the correct address. *"Si, licensiado,"* he said. I collected myself and responded to Judge Cheng and told her Elvis's new address. I grabbed two copies of the blue EOIR-33 and stuck them in Elvis's file. Judge Cheng told me to submit them immediately after the hearing.

At this point, though I had seen master calendar hearings before, I did not know what would happen. I imagined the worst: that I had put Elvis at risk, that Judge Cheng would fashion a unique response based on what she had seen before her. I told myself, if this kept up, my first case could be my last. Drama runs high in immigration law, and immigration lawyers in response slip fluently into melodrama. I was no exception.

Judge Cheng moved on to the pleadings. Like criminal proceedings, immigrants were also "charged" with certain violations of the law in the Notice to Appear (NTA), which was the charging document in immigration proceedings.

"Counsel, are you prepared to plead today?"

"Yes, Your Honor."

Admitting to allegations and conceding that an immigrant was removable did not necessarily limit their access to immigration relief, though some immigration lawyers felt even this was akin to an admission of guilt and they preferred to fight on every charge, admitting nothing. There were debates on which strategy was more appropriate.

NTAs were usually rapid-fire copy-and-paste documents and

if an immigration lawyer found a mistake and wanted to challenge the NTA in court, the lawyer could. In Elvis's case, the charges were straightforward and correct: basically, it said he was from El Salvador, that he entered the United States on or about a certain date at a certain city along the border, and that he was not lawfully present in the United States. With a SIJS case like Elvis's, the pleadings did not matter as much. The NTA was important because immigrants were not technically in removal proceedings until ICE filed the NTA with the immigration court. For example, an immigrant youth would be served with an NTA while in a detention center and then would be released to his or her sponsor. The immigrant youth would not have a court date until the same NTA that ICE gave to the youth was filed with the immigration court that had jurisdiction over the case. In other words, it was yet another waiting period for a person's fate, an uncomfortable indeterminate state.

By the time I started the pleadings, I was feeling as though I had doomed Elvis's chances of staying here. Nonetheless, as I was about to speak, I looked over and caught Elvis's eye. I could see that he was as nervous as I was. We were both new at this, but whereas I was nervous, he was bewildered. The three people speaking—Judge Cheng, the ICE attorney, and me—were deciding his fortunes with little to no input from him. He was along for the ride, so to speak, but he had no idea what this ride entailed. I stopped feeling nervous; his reality interrupted mine and the lesson struck me and stayed with me: I did not know scary, I did not know nervous, until I had walked in Elvis's, or any of the immigrant youths' I worked with, shoes. I must be stronger, I must be better, I told myself. Fortified, I suddenly became fluent, admitting the allegations and conceding removability before respectfully declining to designate a country of removal, just as I had intended to. After that, I informed Judge

Cheng that we were pursuing Special Immigrant Juvenile Status for Elvis and we had just filed his case with USCIS and were awaiting approval. I asked her to administratively close Elvis's case pursuant to *Matter of Avetisyan*, a Board of Immigration Appeals case that allowed immigration judges to administratively close certain proceedings after considering six factors, including the likelihood of success of the SIJS petition we were pursuing with USCIS. Judge Cheng nodded along and then switched gears momentarily. She asked if Elvis was in school and what grade he was in. I turned to look at Elvis, who had not realized that she was addressing him directly. Elvis looked down as he spoke, and the interpreter had to ask him to repeat what he said. He looked at me and I gave him a small smile and a nod. *Cuéntale que sí que vas a la escuela.* Elvis had not been able to go to school for the last three years he had lived in El Salvador. His dream was to become a doctor and though he often showed little emotion, the pride he felt when speaking about attending school again always came through. *Si señora, estoy estudiando ahora, gracias a Dios. Estoy en el grado nueve.*

Judge Cheng looked back at me and quickly gave her valuation, as if it were the most normal thing in the world: Elvis's case was being administratively closed. The ICE attorney objected, and Judge Cheng matter-of-factly told him to file a motion if he was not in agreement. Attorney General Jeff Sessions recently, nearly two years after Elvis's case was administratively closed, stopped this practice with his decision in *Matter of Castro-Tum*, which essentially stripped immigration judges of their power to administratively close cases, even in the interest of judicial efficiency, a decision that would surely serve to only further clog immigration judge's dockets.

"Anything else, Counsel?" she asked, ready to end our hearing.

"No, Your Honor. Thank you."

"Here is the order. Please serve one on the Department."

She handed me two copies of the administrative closure order and I gave one to the ICE attorney. Like the judge, the ICE attorney had been present for every case on the docket that morning—she was in fact the prosecutor for all thirty-five files that she carried in the literal shopping cart that she wheeled into the courtroom. As the cases were called, she would rapidly type the numbers into a thick, ancient laptop and pull the file out of the shopping cart. She likely had no prior idea of the facts of any of the cases, just what she could review quickly on the computer if she were asked a question. Mostly, her job at these hearings consisted in following Department of Homeland Security protocol and policy, like when she automatically objected to administrative closure in Elvis's case. It wasn't Elvis's specific case that made her object; the policy was one of blanket objection to all administrative closures. And so, when ICE attorneys infuriated you, it was like getting upset at a blackjack dealer at the casino: you wrongly assumed they had some control over the terrible hands you were dealt. Still, many ICE attorneys were not just automatons for DHS bureaucracy: unlike a blackjack dealer, they too were playing their cards as best they could.

As we left the courtroom and rode the elevators down to the ground floor, I explained to Elvis what had happened in his case. Even with the interpreter, he confessed that he understood nothing of what went on. This was not rare. A basic theme running through immigration proceedings, more pronounced now than ever, was *We will decide your fate for you.* I assured Elvis that today's hearing was good news and that we would not have to come back to this court. For now, we would simply have to wait on USCIS to issue a decision on his SIJS application.

"Okay, licensiado, gracias."

With that, he turned and walked toward the subway station at City Hall to take the R train back to Brooklyn. It was only noon; there was still half of a school day left. And Elvis, unlike nearly every teenager I have ever met, did not want to miss any more school.

———

Though I represented Elvis in immigration court in Manhattan in removal proceedings, his case began in the Kings County Family Court in Brooklyn, which was where I spent the most time as a lawyer for immigrant youth. Due to our office's location in Brooklyn, many young people who lived in the borough came to us from nearby. For a family court to have jurisdiction over a youth, they must be living in the borough of that family court. Congress—when it was still functioning—decided that the juvenile or family courts, with knowledge and experience dealing with sensitive issues like parental abuse and abandonment, were the proper settings to decide if immigrant youth fit the five requirements needed to make them eligible for SIJS:

1. Under twenty-one years old

2. Unmarried

3. It is not in the best interest of the immigrant youth to return to his or her country of citizenship or last habitual residence

4. The immigrant youth cannot be reunified with one OR both parents due to abuse, abandonment, neglect, or a similar basis under state law (death, imprisonment, etc.)

5. The immigrant youth is under the jurisdiction of a juvenile court

Thus, though family courts could not decide an immigration case, they were the venue where immigration lawyers were tasked with obtaining an initial order evincing that their clients fit the requirements of SIJS. In its most basic form, these requirements served as the initial checklist for immigration lawyers or advocates who screened immigrant youth for potential relief. I knew these five requirements so well that, according to my wife, I would mutter them in my sleep. They were deceptively complex and their interpretations varied by state, with case law and regulations governing the definitions.

If the family or juvenile court judge found that all five requirements for SIJS were met, they would issue an order declaring such, which we would then send, along with a cover letter, fee waiver request, birth certificate, and a dozen other governmental forms to USCIS. This didn't guarantee a youth's relief; rather it was a two-step process where the family court was the goalkeeper and immigration services the referee making all final decisions. A successful application must first pass through the family court. For, as we immigration lawyers were constantly reminded by the government, only immigration services could officially grant or deny immigration status.

Since I did not only represent clients in Brooklyn, I would travel quite regularly to the family courts in the other boroughs as well. The boroughs of New York were for the most part synonymous with its counties, the latter serving as reminders that the State of New York did not treat its eponymous city as one single entity. Therefore, you had New York County (Manhattan), Kings County (Brooklyn), Queens County (Queens), Bronx County (the Bronx), and Richmond County (Staten Island), each one its own world.

In Queens, for example, a borough considered to be the most ethnically diverse urban area on the planet, nearly everyone was or had an immediate relation to an immigrant. It was also, miraculously, the birthplace of President Trump, who was, of course, the son of an immigrant mother. More than eight hundred languages were spoken there, and with some advanced notice to the family court, you could get translators for your case in nearly every one of those languages. This hadn't elicited the sympathies of the Queens County family court judges and referees, however, who were so difficult and unkind to immigrants and advocates that each hearing in front of them felt like a small rebellion against their borough's diversity.

Then there was the often startling, sometimes surreal Bronx County family court where I had witnessed knives pulled, divorced couples with their hands around each other's throats, a father so high that he forgot his child's name, a defendant who tried to relieve himself at the counsel's table, and another father who, to avoid paying child support, used the defense of being his own sovereign nation to argue that U.S. law had no jurisdiction over him.

By contrast, a visit to the family court of Staten Island had a certain reflective and renewing serenity to it. During my first year as an immigration lawyer, the main courthouse for Richmond County family court was under construction, so judges would hear cases in white trailers that gave new meaning to the term "the hallowed halls of justice." Maybe it was the informal setting, but the judge who presided over each one of my cases was fair and understanding. Yet the court and the judge were only part of the experience. Unless one had a car, which I did not, the only way to Staten Island was by taking its iconic (and free) ferry. In the early mornings, while commuters from the island disembarked en masse at the terminal on Manhattan's south shore, I would climb aboard an often deserted ferry heading in the other direction. I would take a seat on its starboard side and stare out the window, contemplating history and the same choppy waters that immigrants crossed to land at Ellis Island all those years ago. Soon, Lady Liberty would come into view—despite myself, each morning that I saw the iconic copper statue, I would absolve the United States in some ways for its sins. A country with a display of that magnitude, with those colossal words inscribed therein, could not be the same one that I saw currently treat its newest arrivals the way it did. Somewhere underneath it all, this promise, the one that she carried, survived. Those twenty floating minutes on the ferry would approximate hope, and I would be so transfixed by this thought that by the time the ferry docked, I would have to rehearse my case notes to return them to my mind.

SIJS cases were not always the strongest avenue for a client, but in many cases, they could be the least triggering. In Celeste's case, she was likely eligible for various forms of immigration relief, yet as Celeste and I spoke, it became clear that she did not have the ability to speak about her past traumas coherently or without shutting down. She would start a sentence *There were four men . . .* and then her chest would seize up and she would begin breathing in short, quick bursts, uncontrollably, as if they were the last breaths she was taking before drowning. It was so visceral that I felt my heart rate accelerate too, believing that I was in the same ocean of sorrows, no longer able to swim either. I tried simple questions, setting up multiple appointments and having her meet with our social worker. Emotional and psychological healing, the support that she desperately needed, took time. But we had no time, not if we were going to apply for SIJS—which I still did not know if she qualified for because our conversations had not resulted in any meaningful exchange of information. She would be turning twenty-one in just under three months and we had not even filed anything in family court yet.

Before one meeting, I told her that I needed to look at any and all paperwork that she had, because I knew that she hoarded these things like tangible memories, and it was part of the reason she could never go beyond her past. She carried a large file folder with her on most days and finally, during that meeting, she let me see what was inside. Everything from police reports, news articles, certificates, photos—I needed to know if I could construct a narrative that could lead to a successful case, because Celeste was not capable of providing one. Based on the information in the folder, I believed Celeste might be able to apply for asylum and perhaps even a T visa. Among these papers, I found a faded death certificate. It was Celeste's father: he had died four years ago. Death was treated differently by all, but it was rarely celebrated. In Celeste's case, without knowing anything else, and for a brief, appalling moment, I was happy: her father's death was a morbid qualifying factor for SIJS, and Celeste could apply for SIJS without having to say much. She would have an opportunity to stay in the United States, hopefully never returning to the place that she could not even speak about.

I spoke with Celeste and explained her case, how she was in removal proceedings and how this avenue of relief was rapidly closing to her. I told her that her father's death would allow us to apply for SIJS, beginning in Kings County Family Court. It helped to have Celeste know what it was we were trying to do and to make sure that it was her decision to go forward in this manner. Transparency allowed trust and cooperation to build between client and attorney, and our organization was committed to it. Because it could be difficult to explain the nuances of immigration law to undocumented youth, however, especially those who spoke little English, this wasn't always an easy thing to provide. For one thing, the degree of difficulty in simplifying legalese in another language without losing the accuracy of the

English meaning was quite high. How would you explain the gradation between "legal guardianship" and "dependency on a juvenile court" in Spanish to adolescents in a way that wouldn't confuse them, so they were not signing up for something they might not be emotionally prepared for, especially when their actual parents were still in their lives? Exacerbating this challenge was the complexities of family dynamics: children who were beaten by their parents often still loved and communicated with their parents; the child was abandoned by a parent due to circumstances outside the parent's control in a civil war–torn nation; and so on. For children of deceased parents, if the child did not have a death certificate, an immigration lawyer needed to obtain a death certificate from whatever office in the youth's country of origin held a record of it. This could easily turn into an adventure of phone calls and a gauntlet of palms wanting to be greased. I once spoke for two hours on the phone with a government official in a small town in Guatemala, spending most of that time trying to convince him to send me a copy of a death certificate without having to pay his "fee" of five hundred dollars. This explained, but did not justify, my passing elation in finding Celeste's father's death certificate in the file folder she carried.

Celeste's case would be heard by Judge Vargas, known for the flamboyant bow ties that peeked out from under his judicial robe. It was normal for him to wear one clothed in silk pink and highlighter yellow or one patterned in turquoise dots above a neon pumpkin orange surface, neckwear that would have been a bold statement on anyone else. Above his robe was a vivaciously groomed head. His naturally dark hair was streaked with blond, perfectly kept and parted to the right. He wore wire-rimmed eyeglasses that were so antiquated-looking, so aggressively out of style, that you began to wonder if maybe they were coming back into style and he knew something you did not. To top it off, he wore them on the tip of his nose, like Chuck Schumer, and I wasn't convinced he needed them for any purpose other than flair. And that was the thing, something about his idiosyncratic style hinted that Judge Vargas was on the side of immigrants and their advocates, and not for nothing did he have a reputation for being the nicest family court judge in New York City. After reading through the SIJS petition and motion I filed for Celeste, which included copies of her father's death certificate, and after hearing her sworn testimony—that I limited to the basics: *Where is your father? When did he die?* and little else to avoid triggering her in open court—he granted an order stating that Celeste qualified for SIJS. Judge Vargas took off his glasses and told Celeste *Buena suerte* as court was adjourned. We had one month left until her twenty-first birthday.

With Judge Vargas's stamp of approval, we quickly mailed USCIS a thick packet of Celeste's SIJS application. This was one of the parts of the job I hated the most. It was impossible to underestimate the ridiculous bureaucracy and bullshit responses that the government seemed to send on a whim. The government usually responded with Requests for Evidence, RFEs as we called them, meaning that they wished to have something clarified or the application was supposedly missing something. I once received seven RFEs in the same week and the language in each RFE was exactly the same, though the cases were wildly different. Sometimes the responses made no applicable sense at all. Imagine if, during an argument with a person regarding whether the North American Free Trade Agreement had spurred undocumented immigration into the United States, they responded with their opinion on the wonderful Mexican produce now available in the United States. This was roughly how the government responded to immigration applications, and increasingly to court cases in general, where it was difficult to continue the argument in any sane or linear fashion.

Still, the RFEs required responses for the case to have a chance at success and we would write responses that were studies in controlled rage and bewilderment, each white-knuckled sentence clenched into a polite disagreement over the merits of what they had stated. *Yes, I understand your stance on the delicious avocado, but I would like to draw your attention to the pertinent points of my client's application.* Because a response could be so infuriating that I'd want to respond *Quit wasting my time, asshole* in the opening paragraph, Becky and I would edit each other's motions and responses for oversteps, with phrases like "Reel it in" or "Pump the brakes" scribbled in the margins whenever annoyance bled through.

Dealing with U.S. Citizenship and Immigration Services was like trying to get a large insurance company to cover your medical bill. *Why was this not covered under my plan?* At which point they would read off an obscure regulation or repeat information that was already on the letter you received. If you had further questions, they would place you on hold to speak with the next level of representative who would be able to assist you better, and on like this, until you hung up in frustration. No one could actually help solve the problem or give you a solution. It was customer service only in name, because as a lawyer, I was not actually their customer—no one was. Interestingly, however, USCIS was entirely self-funded, meaning that they operated wholly on the application fees that immigrants sent with their applications. The Trump administration recently issued a new policy stating that rejected applicants could be given an NTA and put into removal proceedings, heightening the fear of immigrants and advocates and likely driving down the number of applications submitted to USCIS. It remains to be seen if they can continue to operate without these potential fees, without their paying "customers."

That was not to say there weren't good USCIS employees working in our favor on the inside—there were, and it was like being deep undercover—but they tended to be overshadowed by the bad apples. I remembered one woman who answered a call I made regarding a case that had gone beyond normal processing times. It took only an exchange of three sentences to realize she was vehemently anti-immigrant, and another three before she became self-righteous in a way that made her sound like the immigration Kim Davis, the Kentucky county clerk who'd illegally denied a gay couple a marriage license. She shortly thereafter started answering every question I asked with a prim "No." Toward the end, it turned comical.

"May I speak to your supervisor?"

"No."

"May I *please* speak to your supervisor?"

"No."

"Ma'am, I'd thank you kindly to pass me on to your boss."

"No."

"Por favor, puedo hablar con su supervisor?"

"No."

"Do you know what I just said?"

"No."

"I knew it. Come on, you're going to make me call back after a twenty-minute wait on hold?"

"No."

"Do you believe the United States is a nation of immigrants?"

"No."

"Really?"

I suspected she had gotten too carried away with her negative responses to have said anything more encouraging, but she hung up the phone before I could find out. Or perhaps, given that USCIS soon thereafter removed "a nation of immigrants" from its mission statement, she was ahead of the curve on announcing a new policy.

Another phone call with a DHS attorney to get him to join on a motion to reopen the case of a young client of mine revealed that he had only cursory knowledge of the *Perez-Olano* settlement, which, among other things, required him to join my motion since my client had a SIJS approval within the last sixty days. When I read him paragraph twenty-nine of the settlement, where the requirement was explicitly laid out, he simply responded, "Sorry man, I'm not aware of any of that. I won't be joining the motion, but good luck, man!" Of course, immigration lawyers would lose a lot more cases if they took the government at their word. Instead of calling back, I got in touch with his supervisor, and she agreed that the settlement did apply and they were legally obligated to follow it, and so they joined the motion.

This is the essence of being an immigration lawyer. This is who we interact with, this is who decides the approvals or denials, sends out the RFEs, elongating the path to lawful status or obscuring it. These were not anomalous stories. And yet, somehow, some way, immigration lawyers could not be fully adversarial: we needed DHS cooperation on so many cases, and the rules were written to try and force this cooperation and thus spare immigration judges lengthy hearings or further backlog of their docket of cases. If DHS joined a Motion to Reopen, for example, the immigration judge rubber-stamped it. If DHS did not join, it went to an immigration judge and you only had one bite at the apple. But you could work with DHS, see what they disagreed with in the motion, and ask them to join numerous times—negotiating almost, but with heavily skewed bargaining power. If they didn't know about a binding settlement, though, it was hard to find common ground.

All of these characters—from aspiring immigration Kim Davis, to the frat boy lawyer who forgot to do his homework again, to so many others—worked for DHS, the umbrella government agency tasked with executing the outdated and cruel immigration laws. They were simultaneously responsible for protecting the border, enforcement of the laws, deportations, and granting immigration benefits, which included visas for sensitive and traumatic instances, such as asylum or a T visa for a victim of human trafficking. It was as if the United States, once a place known to be open to the world's huddled masses, underwent a remodel and reopened as an exclusive club, where the men and women of DHS were the bouncers, tasked with kicking out the unruly and the unwanted, ensuring that the line into the country was kept long, often turning away those who had spent years waiting in it, and on preciously rare occasions, pulling the velvet rope aside and letting someone in.

———

As I worked on Elvis's case and Celeste's case and dozens of others, President Obama hit an immigration wall of his own: an obstructionist Republican Congress. Throughout his two terms, President Obama used immigrants as bargaining chips in immigration legislation. By indicating that he could be tough on immigration enforcement and border security in both his first and second terms, he hoped to get Republicans to the table to discuss immigration reform. This, of course, included the long-purgatorial Development, Relief, and Education for Alien Minors Act, popularly known as the DREAM Act.

Congressman Luis Gutiérrez first introduced an act to grant a pathway to legal status for undocumented immigrant youth to the House of Representatives in early 2001, and almost immediately, the act was subject to much revision and contention in both the House and the Senate—foreshadowing the next decade of legislative failure. Following a protracted back-and-forth, the DREAM Act, first proposed by the Republican Senator Orrin Hatch, finally emerged as a compromise, but a futile one. Through years of shifting politics and heartbreaking setbacks, the DREAMers (those who would benefit from the DREAM Act) were left to advocate to no avail. It wasn't until June 15, 2012, when the Obama administration acted on the promise of the still unpassed DREAM Act by enacting the Deferred Action for Childhood Arrivals (DACA) policy through Executive Order, that any progress was made. This Executive Order granted undocumented youth brought to the United States before their sixteenth birthday and before June 15, 2007—among other requirements—the ability to apply for a work authorization while also granting them protection from deportation, though without putting them on the path to citizenship like many of the potential DREAM Acts would have done. It was an unstable status, but better than no status. Two years later, in November 2014, President Obama attempted to act again by Executive Order to protect certain eligible immigrants from deportation and grant them a work authorization, with the expansion of the original DACA program and the Deferred Action for Parents of Americans and Lawful Permanent Residents (DAPA) policy, though those policies were soon halted in the courts.

It was this legacy, as a magnanimous risk-taker, alert to the needs of many in the immigrant community, that was so difficult to reconcile with President Obama's aggressive enforcement actions, which had earned him the moniker of "Deporter-in-Chief." For immigrants and their advocates who saw families buoyed by DACA but torn apart by deportations, it was clear that he giveth and he taketh away.

Just after the New Year of 2016, we were vividly reminded of what it meant to take away. Our office had just reopened after a two-week break, and a holiday spirit lingered in the air, or so I thought. New Year's Day had landed on a Friday, meaning we didn't return to the office until the fourth of January. The office was freezing, but we warmed it quickly with our excitement. The frost on the windows didn't bother anyone once we were together again. At a staff meeting on our first day back, we shared hot chocolate and swapped descriptions of gifts—the great ones and the duds—the massive family meals, the exotic or quiet getaways, and, of course, our resolutions for the new year. Some of my co-workers had spent those two weeks outside of the city, like we had, visiting family or vacationing someplace warm. I spoke contentedly about our daughter's first Christmas—her eyes lit up by the Christmas tree lights, knee-deep in scraps of wrapping paper—and our wedding anniversary, which was on New Year's Eve.

But the idle was short-lived. Over the weekend, ICE officials had begun an aggressive operation to apprehend immigrants, arresting scores of people before we had even unlocked our doors. Our answering machines were full of messages from concerned clients. Through dozens of Know-Your-Rights trainings in the last year, we had coached many undocumented immigrants on how to deal with an immigration raid. But the early reports from North Carolina, Georgia, and Texas, where the first raids had taken place, depicted a more ruthless and efficient ICE let loose on an unsuspecting population just hours removed from fireworks and the elation of a new beginning. ICE was using surprise tactics to get the undocumented immigrants they had on their list, as well as anyone unlucky enough to be in the wrong place at the wrong time.

The office catapulted into work. That day, we heard, more raids were being planned. We set up a list of immigrant youth to call and a prerecorded script to explain what was happening and encouraged them to put anyone they knew in touch with us. National Public Radio reported on the raids and called our office asking for permission to broadcast the script, and even taped me making a call to an undocumented youth. An unsuspecting audience who had no such fears as ICE raids would have their afternoons interrupted with this news.

According to advocates in our network and later an announcement by DHS, the immigration raids were targeted at undocumented immigrants with a deportation order, criminal records, or recent arrivals from the previous summer. The announcement, like many I had read before and heard in political stump speeches or seen throughout history, was a skillful framing to allay liberal guilt: *We are not doing anything wrong, only getting rid of the undesirables.* Hardly anyone would be perturbed when ICE went after *criminal* immigrants. And yet, it was impossible to predict whose door ICE would come pounding on. Their methods and their announcements never jived; half the story, at least and sometimes more, was never told. Much of what we knew regarding immigration raids was after-the-fact. ICE operated with guerrilla tactics and vast resources that kept immigrants and advocacy organizations in the dark, quite literally. At 5:00 a.m.: loud banging on the door, before the kids left for school, before the first alarm sounded, before the sun even rose. Home, the only sanctuary that many of us had, was constantly violated by ICE. Under President Obama, there was a DHS memorandum that guided ICE officers and explicitly told them to avoid sensitive areas while conducting raids, including schools. Under President Trump, the memorandum was rescinded. Any place was now a good place for an immigration raid.

On that first morning back from the holiday, hot chocolate still in our stomachs, it was the brutal reality of ICE that would come knocking at our door. Dozens of youths arrived at our office, concerned and frightened. Just as we had prerecorded a script, we had letters signed by Becky or myself, stating that we were currently assisting these youth in applying for immigration relief or evaluating their cases and that ICE should not speak to them without us present. This wasn't true for everyone, and there were a handful of youth we had not even seen before, brought by their friend or sibling, but ICE wouldn't know that. We handed them out to as many people as we could and told them to keep the letter with them. We thought it would work; at the very least, it was a security blanket for the immigrant youth scared to step outside.

Nuria, an undocumented immigrant youth from Honduras who, at twenty years old, lived in Staten Island with her younger brother and his girlfriend, had left messages on our phone that we did not hear until around 10:00 a.m. She showed up at our office with her brother and his girlfriend an hour later, terrified, sure that ICE would pick them up on the ferry, on the subway, on the walk up to our office. Before dawn, ICE had showed up at their house in Staten Island, knocked heavily on the door saying they were police. Nuria's brother had looked through the peephole and spotted ICE insignias. He ran back to his bedroom and told Nuria to stay in hers. After being defrauded by a *notario* whom she had paid to represent her, Nuria had not been informed of her hearing and was ordered removed *in absentia* after failing to appear at a hearing she knew nothing about. Having a removal order was like having a "bounty on your head" bulletin posted during the time of the Wild West. After the *notario* disappeared and Nuria concluded that she had been scammed, she and her brother had come to us, where we discovered the removal order. Because she had been ordered removed, we were concerned that Nuria might be a priority for ICE, even before the newest round of raids began. I was working on getting her removal order rescinded and her case reopened, but I had reiterated to her several times what to do in case an ICE officer showed up at their home. If ICE came to their home, her brother and his girlfriend, untargeted yet undocumented, could also be picked up, a spate of misfortune that happens too often. That is why the Spanish translation of the word we were using—*redadas*, meaning "webs"—to describe the raids in our prerecorded scripts was perhaps a more accurate description of the immigration actions of ICE. A web did not discriminate in what it caught.

For those concerned that Facebook and Twitter were building an Orwellian world where everyone's movement would be mapped and known, such a reality had long existed for undocumented immigrants. Their interactions with DHS were Big Brother come to fruition. Not every detail of a person's life was known, of course, but what was unknown was masked and minimized by rumors spread among the immigrant community, by imagination and by fear. The result was a large population of undocumented immigrants who were unable to have a normal engagement with society. I have been asked why undocumented immigrants didn't interact more with the community, why instead they chose to live, for the most part, in the shadows. It was because there was no genuinely safe interaction for an undocumented immigrant. Signing a lease, opening a bank account, getting an ITIN number to pay taxes, signing up for ID

NYC—anything where a name and address must be included, in the mind of an undocumented immigrant, had the potential to end up in DHS's hands. This extended further as well. Undocumented immigrants, for example, were loath to call the police. I worked with a young undocumented man who called the police when his father was beating his mother, and his father ended up in immigration detention and eventually deported following criminal proceedings relating to that incident. It tore apart an already unstable family and there were arguments, from the outside looking in, that perhaps they were better off without the father, without domestic violence. But, to prove the point of the level of mistrust among undocumented immigrants and law enforcement, his mother was most upset at him for breaking the undocumented family rule: never call the police. Calling the police had put all three of them at risk, and they were lucky that only the father was deported.

This consequence was heightened during the Obama years, when his administration launched the Secure Communities program, which opened a pipeline of information from local law enforcement straight to DHS and its police force, ICE. Anyone who had gotten ticketed for something as inane as driving without a license—which, because many states did not allow undocumented immigrants access to a driver's license, meant thousands of immigrants—would then have their information passed on to ICE, so that they would either be held in jail until they were transferred directly to an immigration detention center, or else be released from jail and sometime later, maybe a few hours, maybe two weeks, maybe a month, ICE would come raid their home. It was only after intense public criticism that President Obama rescinded or renamed the program—depending on who you talk to. From this was born the Sanctuary City movement, where cities would announce that they were a "sanctuary" for undocumented immigrants, which meant that local law enforcement in such a place would not be sharing the information of undocumented immigrants with ICE. It was a powerful gesture, but also largely symbolic in many ways. New York City had long been a sanctuary city and has some of the strongest sanctuary protections, and yet, five hours after ICE first knocked on their door, Nuria and her brother and his girlfriend were all sitting in our office, distraught and terrified to go home.

Nuria told us how, when ICE started banging on the door, she had hidden under her bed. I imagined her in this universal hiding place, as if the cozy squeeze of being under a bed could give her the temporary assurance of comfort or perceived protection. It was one of the first hiding places we discovered as children, and in moments of fear as adults, we often returned to it. The ICE agents left after ten minutes or so, but Nuria stayed under her bed until she thought it was safe to get out. She went into her brother's room, where he and his girlfriend were hugging each other tightly, trying not to breathe too loudly. They cried silently together. The three of them stayed there for another hour before crawling to the window and looking outside. Seeing no ICE officers, they anxiously decided to strike out for our office.

Nuria and her brother and his girlfriend left our office that day and did not know where to go. They talked about never going back to their house, about staying at our office in Casa or moving somewhere else that very day. They stayed with friends for a few nights before eventually returning home, reasoning that ICE must have forgotten about them by now.

But that was not the case. Only a week after they had come to us, ICE showed up again at Nuria's house. She was at work and her brother had just stepped out, leaving his girlfriend home alone when ICE arrived. Instead of hiding, she answered the door, assuming it was Nuria's brother returning, having forgotten his key. She was immediately arrested and taken to a detention center in New Jersey. Nuria felt terrible, as if it was her fault, as if there was a tracking device on her that had led ICE directly to their home. If she hadn't lived there, her brother's girlfriend would not be in detention, she reasoned.

Her brother, at least outwardly, did not blame her.

It was this country that took her from me, he told her, not you.

———

Three months later, the immigration legacy of President Obama was facing its final referendum. By announcing two new policies in November 2014—one an expansion to his already Republican-contested DACA policy, and the other a new policy known as Deferred Action for Parents of Americans and Lawful Permanent Residents (DAPA) that would allow for permanent residents and parents of U.S. citizens to apply lawfully for a work authorization and protection from deportation—President Obama seemed to seek absolution. Meanwhile, the raids and deportations of thousands of undocumented immigrants originally meant to assuage the GOP continued unabated.

Almost immediately, the two new policies were met with heavy resistance by Republicans. Twenty-six states, led by Texas, filed a lawsuit, claiming that President Obama had overstepped the bounds of presidential power and ignored administrative procedures for changing rules. After hearing preliminary arguments, District Court Judge Andrew Hanen, ironically sitting in Brownsville, Texas, issued a preliminary injunction in February 2015, a ruling that effectively stopped the two policies from being implemented. President Obama's Department of Justice appealed the injunction to the Fifth Circuit Court of

Appeals and that court in November 2015 affirmed the Brownsville injunction. The Obama administration again appealed that
decision to the Supreme Court of the United States on grounds
that mandating immigration policy was within the scope of the
executive branch of government. In January of 2016, as Nuria
and her brother sat in my office crying and the chorus of public
protest to the raids grew to a clamor, the Supreme Court granted
certiorari—meaning it agreed to take the case and review the
Fifth Circuit's decision. The case, now called *United States
v. Texas*, was set for oral arguments on April 18 of that year.

A month after the Supreme Court agreed to hear the case, the
conservative bulldog Justice Antonin Scalia passed away, which
at the time, and with no disrespect to the deceased, seemed like
a blessing for the case. Led by the brilliant Scalia, the conservative wing of the Supreme Court had long held a slim 5–4 majority, and it seemed very likely that this case would fall victim to
this conservative majority. The possibility that President Obama
would be able to appoint a justice of his choosing, eleven months
before leaving office and, hopefully, before oral arguments on
the DAPA/DACA+ (the plus sign indicating DACA's expansion)
case, had many immigrants and advocates like myself feeling
hopeful.

This, of course, did not happen. President Obama selected
Judge Merrick Garland as Scalia's replacement on March 16,
2016. As the chief judge of the U.S. Court of Appeals in the
District of Columbia Circuit, Garland was a more mainstream
and middle-of-the-road liberal than most of us wanted, but a
compromise option with unimpeachable credentials that, in
past Congresses where bipartisanship existed, would have flown
through confirmation. Instead, Republican senators, holding a
majority of seats in the Senate and led by infamously conservative Mitch McConnell, refused to hold a hearing or vote on

Garland, arguing that the next president should be the one to fill the seat. The 5–4 conservative majority became a 4–4 split for the foreseeable future. Like in sports, when there would be a tie within the law, nothing was settled. Nobody would win the case, but somebody—and sometimes everybody—lost.

It was a unique and messy case, unprecedented even, with generational consequences. As if to confirm this, the Supreme Court, which usually split sixty minutes between the two sides arguing before it, instead expanded oral arguments in this case, allowing ten extra minutes for a lawyer representing a group of immigrant women who would have benefited from DAPA/DACA+ and fifteen minutes to the Republican-controlled U.S. House of Representatives. The law might seem tributary—politics, undeniably, were playing a leading role in this case.

Such was the state of anxiety on the morning of the argument that electrified the passengers, including myself, on a bus bound for Washington, DC. The refusal of the Senate to consider Garland's nomination was secondary—we were heading to D.C. for the millions who would benefit from the DACA expansion and DAPA—but it was also inescapable. In our minds, the ravages of this case being filed to stop the two immigration policies from going forward in the first place was now part and parcel of the indignity of it being heard before only eight justices. A protest was planned for the day, with many advocacy groups banding around the court hearing of *United States v. Texas*, to create as large an impact as possible.

Our bus—one of three leaving from New York City to attend the rally—was part of a mobilization group assembled by the New York Immigration Coalition, one of the city's largest immigration advocacy groups. Though two of my colleagues were along for the ride, the seat next to me was unfilled. It seems no one wanted to sit next to a six-foot-six beanstalk with inconveniently long legs that unfolded out into the aisle. Dozens of undocumented immigrants, all of whom would have qualified for DAPA or the DACA expansion filled the rows in front of and behind us and remained quiet and shy for the ride down. Nearly every one of them carried the stoic look of people going into battle. They had been talked about in the abstract, as *illegal aliens*, for so long, and joining this rally had made everything more real for them—and hopefully for the justices deciding their fate—which, I think, was the point of them being on the bus and at this rally. A young woman sitting nearby was being shadowed by a reporter with a handheld camera. She had a small microphone pinned to her shirt. She qualified for DACA's expansion, having missed the arrival-date requirement of the original DACA by less than a year. She was in her last year of high school and had been accepted to numerous colleges in the city. Across the aisle from her and two rows in front of me a young boy, who might have been the younger brother of the woman, was reading *Harry Potter and the Goblet of Fire*. He had brought along the hardcover version, a seven-hundred-plus-page tome, and if it weren't for his inclusion on this bus, nothing would have set him apart from the millions of other children who had excitedly read the book.

After a stop somewhere in Delaware for restrooms and breakfast, we were back on the bus, and the organizers began handing out our boxed lunches. Several people had brought materials to make signs, and numerous T-shirts were passed out as well—I got an extra-large white T-shirt that read *protege el amor* in black letters, with a red heart for the o in *Amor*, and a red-and-white-striped sign that said KEEP FAMILIES TOGETHER. The last thirty minutes before arriving in D.C. were spent rehearsing chants and going over logistics. We parked and got out at a church on Second and East Capitol.

By the time we arrived at the rally, speakers were already going, including two executive directors from immigrant organizations in New York, as well as New York City Council member Carlos Menchaca, the leader of the City Council's Immigration Committee and the representative from the district where our organization was located. I stood in the crowd as Menchaca was wrapping up, just in time to applaud as he made his way off the platform. I awaited another speaker, but instead there was a call to begin marching toward the Supreme Court, just down the street from where we were at that moment. It was a Monday, but there was still a large crowd, many of them with bobbing signs in their hands. All of us were chanting.

> *El Pueblo Unido . . . Jamás Sera Vencido*
> *Si se puede! . . . Si se puede! . . .*
> *What do we want? DAPA! When do we want it? NOW!*

Family was the broad theme of the day—KEEP FAMILIES TOGETHER was plastered on signs and shirts throughout the crowd. I wondered as I saw the signs bearing this message if this wasn't couching the issue in Republican terms, convincing the majority party, the supposed family values party, that breaking up parents and children via deportation could or should equate to divorce or abortion. Doing so would assume that conservatives value the idea of family as sacrosanct, even if all of a family's members, individually, are labelled wholly unhuman, as *illegal* and *aliens*. Asking that values and beliefs apply equally to all members of society was not, however, a strong suit of the Republican party, or the United States generally for that matter. And yet the majority of people in attendance were undoubtedly families. Fathers with babies strapped to their chests; toddlers with one hand in their mothers' palms, the other holding tiny

American flags; teenagers not in school because today mattered as much as Election Day, because protesting was as American as voting. These were families as American as apple pie, the only difference being that not all members of the family could eat it without having to look over their shoulder.

The Supreme Court came into view in all its marbled, neo-classical glory. I had been here once before, back when my interest in law was still burgeoning. I had been intimidated by the imposing building then, and I was intimidated by it now. A black lamp hung down over the bronze doors, and on the ground on either side of it were statues, one titled *The Authority of Law* and the other *The Contemplation of Justice*. Before them were massive pillars holding up an intricately engraved western façade with Grecian figures squeezed into the pediment. Directly below their feet the words Equal Justice Under the Law—admittedly more of an aspiration than a truth—were engraved. Its white steps seemed to float upward, like a road that ended at the gates of heaven, which the large bronze front doors emulated convincingly. Thinking of heaven caused me to remember the basketball court on the fifth floor of the building, truly the highest court in the land—and though its existence would seem absurd, I would love to play there. But it was not likely that many of the people with me knew about this other court. Rather what was visible was that we were before a truly supreme court, a place where millions of lives could be changed in one hearing, with one decision. On this day, for millions of undocumented immigrants, the possibility was palpable.

The holy steps, the ones that led up to the building's entrance, were fenced off. The protest would remain here until a few hours later, when a trickle of immigrants and their lawyers came out of the building, clasping their hands together and holding them high above their heads to a raucous cheer from the crowd. For a moment, they looked like miniature people shrunk from the grand building behind them, but their spirit and the energy of the crowd grew them into giants. The Supreme Court no longer seemed intimidating: we had imposed our will on it, or so it seemed then.

Joining us in front of the court were advocacy groups from across the country: the United Farm Workers, the California-based labor group founded by Cesar Chavez; CASA from Maryland, a progressive and influential nonprofit that provided numerous resources for undocumented immigrants across the state; and United We Dream, the largest immigrant youth organization in the country. Even a multifaith group—with rabbis, priests, ministers—bearing signs that read FAITH FOR FAMILIES had joined us. Chants rose and fell, each organization launching their own, until everyone caught the flow and the chants became uniform and shared, hundreds of people deep. Only when the speeches started did the voices die down.

The New Jersey senator Bob Menendez came up to the podium to defend the lawfulness of executive orders. Menendez had been indicted on corruption charges exactly a year before, and his appearance was, at least to me, more surprising than galvanizing. Representative Joaquin Castro, one of the few Texas congressman voted in as a Democrat, was more eloquent in addressing the contributions Latinos have made on behalf of America. The Pulitzer Prize–winning journalist and immigration rights activist Jose Antonio Vargas spoke passionately about being an undocumented immigrant. An undocumented woman with two U.S.–citizen children spoke of the need for immigration reform and her hopes for this case and being able to apply for DAPA. Fighting for air space was the much smaller and strikingly less diverse rally organized by the Federation for American Immigration Reform (FAIR) and, at least initially, focused on the nomination of Merrick Garland. Their podium was adjacent to our own. Their first speaker explained that the Senate was doing the right thing in not even considering Garland's nomination. Activists from our rally, which was orchestrated on a national level by the Fair Immigration Reform Movement (FIRM), a pro-immigrant group, were all too happy to shout and jeer as each FAIR speaker took to the podium. Still, they continued to speak, and in their frustration, the ingrained beliefs of each FAIR speaker came to the fore. What began as a protest to Garland's nomination moved to anti-immigration and anti-DAPA/DACA+, anti-anything pro-immigrant, all met with much louder rebuke. Several FAIR speakers left the podium with faces reddened from trying to shout angrily above our crowd.

As the speeches went on and the groups got to know one another, I felt what my mother has felt as an immigrant to this country, why she believed this was the greatest country in the world: a vast love for the spirit, for the ability to protest and critique the country and the ample space for effecting change, something that had been crushed in her during the military coup in Chile and was reborn here. I felt what the people around me felt, inspired and defiant. This was a true representation of America, no matter what decision came through the bronze doors, in front of this hallowed building where separate was found to be unequal in *Brown v. Board of Education* and where we hoped the same impediments that have prevented so many people from living out the American Dream would be wiped away.

Two months later, with an even eight justices, the opinion issued by the court was as apathetic as it was unsurprising:

The judgment is affirmed by an equally divided court.

That was it. No saucy twenty-page dissent from Justice Clarence Thomas, the lone conservative ranger. No illuminating, passionate plea from Justice Ruth Bader Ginsburg, the liberal lion. Just a 4–4 split; a nondecision. No precedent, no relief, just an affirmation of one district court judge's decision in Brownsville, Texas, to block an Executive Order. Merrick Garland would be kept waiting on the sidelines, and joining him would be the millions of people that might have qualified for DAPA/DACA+.

When the ruling was announced, most of my colleagues were agonized but not surprised. It was, after all, the most likely outcome. Some, however, had been optimistic, predicting Justice Kennedy would swing to our side, as he had on the marriage equality case. Or even Chief Justice Roberts, forever focused on issues of "standing" and the legitimacy of the court, would cast the deciding vote, keeping the court clear of partisan politics. We all agreed that Garland would have been the fifth vote.

Everyone saw the ruling as a setback, but not the end. The ruling was just on the injunction. The merits—the actual case—would still need to be heard in Texas district court and could theoretically eventually work its way back up to the Supreme Court for a full hearing. By then, we would have the first female president in the history of the United States, and Garland, or perhaps someone even more liberal, would be confirmed as the ninth justice on the Supreme Court.

We all know how that turned out. Instead, on June 15, 2017, exactly five years after President Obama signed the original DACA Executive Order, in what I can only imagine was a purposefully timed and pointed statement, the Trump administration rescinded the expanded DACA and DAPA memorandums, striking the final nail into the coffin of a policy that could have helped millions.

In retrospect, we should have seen what was happening. It

was more than a ruling; it was a sign of the times. On that April day, we might have been chanting, marching, fists in the air and standing in solidarity across state lines, immigration status, gender, age—all of us in front of the white steps and white pillars of the highest court in the United States. We might have been jubilant on the bus ride back, as if our activism could somehow make a difference, spring a ninth justice from congressional lockdown, swing a conservative justice's vote, or enter the hearts and minds of eight men and women with the fate of millions resting on their next words. I would like to think we weren't naive, that there was something unwritten that we could help write. Yet on June 23, two short months after our stirring protest at the Supreme Court, the future appeared, and it was nine words long. One sentence from a divided court foreshadowing our divided nation.

PART II

HOME

. . . .

Because *homeland* is one of the magical fantasy words like *unicorn* and *soul* and *infinity* that have now passed into language.

—*Zadie Smith*, White Teeth

1

Of the reasons I can think of as to why I became an immigration lawyer—career-altering mentors, the rapid rise of anti-immigrant sentiment, the pressing need for bilingual Spanish speakers—at the heart of this decision lay my mother's own immigrant story.

A lifetime ago, my mother left her native Chile for the United States. Through her husband at the time, an American living in Santiago, she became a permanent resident and then a citizen. The years passed, and as Chile receded further and further away from her, she came to the realization that her dream of returning had been permanently deferred. *Home*, the word, the concept, the tactile, always held a mournful significance for her. I remember the day she calculated that she had lived longer in the United States than in Chile.

She would often discuss this with me and my father, her second husband, as if maintaining an internal debate about what was home to her kept a flame alive. And then she stopped keeping vigil over it, striking home from her mind, she told us, because home, she realized, was just a word, one that could warm the heart or be used to hurt it. Home was a myth, she told me, no different than the myth of the homeland. When people shouted at an immigrant to "go home," they were building an idea of homeland that overshadowed that long-held American ideal, that this was a nation of immigrants.

She would often cite the writer Jean Rhys, from a passage in *Smile Please*, her unfinished autobiography. She called it the immigrant refrain, and in her unapologetic self-taught English, she would quote: *I would never really belong anywhere, and I knew it, and all my life would be the same, trying to belong, and failing.* My mother shared these thoughts, as she often did, in the form of a monologue, speaking through her feelings as she worked to understand them, a habit I had always known her to have. It made her a great speaker at immigrant rights rallies, and her advocacy work was something she put her heart and soul into. I remember how she once traveled from Reno, where we were based, to Los Angeles, so she could then catch one of eighteen buses of the Immigrant Workers Freedom Ride. The convoy was to cross the entire country ending at Flushing Meadows in Queens, New York, and she would be with them, on the bus, for every mile.

Activism had long been in my mother's blood. In Chile, as a spirited college student, she had been spellbound by Salvador Allende, a Socialist doctor running for president. My mother worked on his campaign, attended his rallies, and went with fellow supporters to cast decisive votes in the 1970 presidential election in which he would claim victory. Three years later, on September 11, 1973, Salvador Allende lay dead from a controversial gunshot wound in the presidential palace. The military junta, led by General Augusto Pinochet, came swiftly to power, and to keep it, Pinochet's troops began systematically torturing, "disappearing," and killing in plain sight as many of Allende's supporters as they could find. For four months, my mother feared for her life until, in January of 1974, my mother's first husband was able to get her out of Chile and into the United States of America. She was a different person after that, she has told me; everyone that is forced to emigrate leaves a part of themselves behind. Though she had suspected it, it was only after she naturalized and swore allegiance to the flag, that she confirmed that Americans had invested money and sent CIA operatives to Santiago in order to help Pinochet plan and execute his coup.

My mother has an astonishing ability to recall her departure from her native country, and after telling myself that I would one day do so, I eventually worked up the courage to ask if she might let me interview her. This was years after I had left home, graduated from college, was practicing as an immigration lawyer, and had a family. I wanted to have a record of her story, but also I wanted to hear firsthand what it meant for her to leave her beloved Chile. Selfishly, I hoped it would help me to better understand the immigrants I was representing. By that time, I had come to learn the first rule of immigration: people do not immigrate to the United States simply seeking a better life, but often to escape one much worse. It was formal, speaking to my mother as though a journalist, but she took it in stride. When I clicked on record and asked her to relate her memories of that time, she answered with loquacity, as though I had uncorked something long bottled up.

2

From an interview with my mother about the morning of September 11, 1973, when General Augusto Pinochet led a successful coup against the elected president, Salvador Allende.

"I usually had calm mornings with coffee and reading before my classes. But on the day Pinochet took power, there was no coffee and no reading. The sounds of gunshots were everywhere and I remember them most vividly. My father owned a few guns that he hunted with on his property in Rancagua, and he had a handgun in the house that he shot off once during an argument. Until then, those were the only gunshots I'd ever heard. But on that day, I heard bullets leaving so many rifles. One gunshot was close enough to where I was that I heard the sound of a bullet hitting something soft. I didn't know what it had struck.

"My brother had died just a few months earlier. He had been in a terrible car accident and the hospital workers, divided like the rest of Chile, had gone on strike against a faltering economy led by Allende's attempts to socialize it. No one could locate any intravenous fluid for my brother since the only factory in the city that produced it was also on strike. I have always wondered if he would have survived under different circumstances. My mother had gone to Mendoza, Argentina, where she was from, to be with her sisters and grieve. My father was off with Maria, one of his lovers, the first one that had finally convinced him to leave my mother. My sister had moved to Venezuela with her husband a year earlier. I was alone in the house. I didn't know what was happening.

"We lived on Tegualda street, in the new Barrio Italia as they called it, not far from La Moneda—the presidential palace—and downtown Santiago. We had an old house with an interior courtyard, like you see in Spain; it was beautiful, especially in summer. Yet an interior courtyard was impractical during the winter, when Santiago gets very cold, and you'd have to venture outdoors just to get from one room to another.

"There had been rumors in the last few weeks—months even, I guess. The CIA was around. Americans started popping up all over Santiago. There were forty-year-old undergraduates at the university 'studying,' and people that spoke no Spanish were photographing the most innocuous events and claiming to be 'journalists' but never stating who they worked for. It was strange and obvious, but what could we do? I met an American that was in the Peace Corps and he was a bit old for it. The Peace Corps was still new, but everyone loved the volunteers because they felt connected to Kennedy, a man we all loved, in some way. We started dating. My friends thought that he was CIA too, but he never seemed like it and he never admitted it to me. We got married two months before September 11, but that's another story. He was in the south, hiking on that day—another clue, my friends said later—and I didn't want to go when he invited me. He loved the outdoors and I was a city girl.

"At 6:00 a.m. that Tuesday morning, September 11, the phone rang, and I answered it. My father's voice came through on the other side. Don't go to school today, he said. He was a politician, tight with Chile's right wing. He blamed Allende for my brother's death, but it was his political party that was leading many of the protests and strikes against the Allende government. My father knew something was happening. On the phone, he said he couldn't tell me what exactly was happening, but he said a revolution was coming. I have never heard that word so misused in my life.

"I did not like my father and I had stopped listening to what he told me once I started university. I loved my classes, though, so the opportunity to disobey my father and go to class was right up my alley. After showering, I turned on the radio. Military music played triumphantly. The military men that came on told everyone to stay in their homes. They said the military had moved in and surrounded La Moneda, the presidential palace, and taken over the ports. I didn't believe it, and I also didn't know which military they meant.

"I heard airplanes overhead and some loud explosions. Gunshots rang out sporadically. I thought maybe it was the Americans or even the Soviets. It was the Cold War then, and you assumed one country or the other was involved in most things that happened. The Chilean military had pledged their loyalty to Allende recently, Pinochet especially. It never crossed my mind that Chile was attacking Chile. But then, little by little, the news started to come in. Our military had turned on Allende and were taking over. The generals, Pinochet and others, had betrayed Allende. They had all the weapons, all the might.

"The gunshots got closer. People in the street were screaming. Someone banged on my neighbor's door and then kicked it in. I heard gunshots against their roof and it echoed in the courtyard of our house. I ran and locked the door, then ran back into my room and hid under my bed. I held my breath, for one minute, then two. I heard footsteps. The houses were so close together that it was difficult to tell if they were on our property, on our doorsteps, or at another neighbor's house. They never came to our door.

"I got out from under my bed after an hour or so. The phone rang again. It scared me. I answered it, so the noise would stop, then realized someone outside would know I was home if I answered. I didn't speak. The voice on the other end was familiar. It was my father, again. He told me to not leave the house, to hide if they knocked on our doors. He said the phones were tapped and to not call any of my friends, all of whom he knew were leftist and Allende supporters. He said they were searching homes and taking people. I said nothing. I hung up. I started to look around my bedroom at all the leftist books and music, the Allende poster on the wall. Any military officer that came into my room would detain me immediately.

"I turned on the radio where it was announced that those loyal to the military coup should put Chilean flags outside their homes. I didn't do it. It was my dangerous resistance. Alone in my house, I felt more frightened and more powerful at the same time. I closed the windows to avoid seeing the atrocities going on outside. There were dead in the streets now, and bodies were floating in the Mapocho River that crosses Santiago, not far from our house. I turned to another channel on the radio and there was silence, and then Salvador Allende started speaking. He started speaking right around eight in the morning and spoke a few times, four in all, with the last time being after nine. I'll never forget his last words. I recorded them with a tape recorder I had, which I had used to record all of my history lectures at the university. This was actually history, though, and as Allende spoke of himself in the past tense, I began to weep."

My mother stops and asks me to look up Allende's last words, which I read to her.

Trabajadores de mi patria: tengo fe en Chile y su destino. Superarán otros hombres este momento gris y amargo, donde la traición pretende imponerse. Sigan ustedes sabiendo que, mucho más temprano que tarde, de nuevo abrirán las grandes alamedas por donde pase el hombre libre para construir una sociedad mejor.

¡Viva Chile! ¡Viva el pueblo! ¡Vivan los trabajadores!

Éstas son mis últimas palabras y tengo la certeza de que mi sacrificio no será en vano. Tengo la certeza de que, por lo menos, habrá una lección moral que castigará la felonía, la cobardía y la traición.*

---

*Workers of my country: I have faith in Chile and its destiny. Other men will overcome this gray and bitter moment, where the betrayal tries to impose itself. Keep on knowing that, much sooner rather than later, you

"Those words still give me chills. It's like he is still alive and I'm still twenty-three when I hear them. Pinochet announced that they were giving Allende an opportunity to leave the country. The military broadcast this on other radio stations. They gave Allende a deadline, then another and another, even offering to escort him out of the country by helicopter. Allende would not accept the offer; he was going to stay until the end, testing how far Pinochet was willing to wait until he forced the military to act. Finally, I heard the roar of airplanes. The ground seemed to shake. I didn't know what was happening until I heard explosions, one after the other, louder and louder. It felt like they were blowing up all of Santiago. It was only later that I learned that they had bombed the presidential palace, with Allende and two people loyal to him inside. They say Allende killed himself—and to drive home the communist connection, with a gun that Fidel Castro gave him—but I don't think he did. Why would he stay until the very end, denying every offer of exile, and then kill himself? If he was going to make the ultimate sacrifice, I believe, he would make the military do it for him."

On leaving Chile for the United States and learning to call it home.

"They wouldn't let anyone leave their houses for three days, and I had nothing to eat but old, stale bread. There was smoke everywhere. The smoke felt like it was rising from a fire that was

---

will again open the great avenues where the free man passes to build a better society. Long live Chile! Long live the people! Long live the workers! These are my last words and I am certain that my sacrifice will not be in vain. I am certain that, at least, there will be a moral lesson that will punish felony, cowardice and betrayal.

put out: they had killed the last dream of democracy in Chile. Within that smoke was the ashes of our hopes.

"When I finally left the house and was able to see Michael, my husband at the time, we didn't immediately talk about leaving. He was in love with Chile—more so the country than me even, I think—and I could not leave my mother alone, not so quickly after my brother had died. We decided to wait. It was a risk.

"There was a curfew instituted, and we couldn't be out past a certain hour or else the soldiers on patrol would pick you up. We didn't know where they were taking people. Lots of houses on our street were empty. People had left or been taken. By then we knew that Allende was dead. No one knew where his body was. They had taken it away and buried it secretly. Only years later would he receive a proper burial. We started to hear other things too. There were thousands of people being kept at the Estadio Nacional. I had seen Fidel Castro and Allende speak together two years earlier at the Estadio Nacional. Someone said that Victor Jara, Chile's Bob Dylan, was being kept there. Two weeks later Pablo Neruda, my hero, died, but the military tried to keep it a secret—I think they killed him too, or else he died of a broken heart, seeing his beloved Chile in this state. People were disappearing, leaving the country or floating in the bloodred river. Congress was shut down. The courts were too. Pinochet appeared on the radio and on television, referring to himself as El Jefe de la Junta. He controlled all of the press.

"The military closed my university. They made all of us students re-register and apply to be reinstated. I was scared to go, but my father—who was happy that Allende had been removed, which made me even sicker to my stomach when speaking to him—assured me that I would be okay if I went to the university on the designated date. He knew more about the new regime than I did, so for once I listened to him. Military officers were waiting in front of the university buildings, checking our IDs to see who we were and if we could go back to school. After they checked my ID, an officer began frisking me. He grabbed my breasts firmly several times and did the same to my butt. The military was in charge and they wanted everyone to know it. No one could touch them, but they could touch everybody. I found out later that many of the university people were destroying documents as the coup happened, to protect the students. I went because I was only three months away from graduating, and I wanted to get my degree. I didn't think they'd stop me from finishing. But I was in the history department, and we were very active and leftist. I had campaigned for Allende, and most of my colleagues [had] too. They made an announcement a few weeks after we checked in at the university that only two students from the history department would be allowed to continue. I wasn't one of them and I didn't recognize their names. Later I found out that those two students were from before the Allende years, and they had never finished their studies; only because they had missed the period of political activism on campus were they reinstated.

"My two best friends that came with me to re-register didn't stay around and wait for the announcement. When I called their houses, no one answered. Still, today, all these years later, I don't know what became of them. That was the way with many of us. It wasn't until Facebook came around that I was able to regain contact with a few people. Someone from the history department broached the idea of having a reunion a few years ago, but it never happened. Everyone thought it would be too sad—not to see each other again, but to see the ghosts: to finally know who was missing.

"So I never went back to the university again. Because they

didn't let me back in to the university, it was clear that they had me on some list or knew something about my political activity. Five years of university. Gone. I wasn't going to be a professor. Not in Chile at least.

"My mother was the only reason I was still in Chile. In our culture, you left your parents' house when you got married, and then it was only to move next door or across the street. Once I realized that I couldn't finish my degree, it was harder to stay. We decided to pack everything and go to the U.S. It was the hardest thing I have ever done. My mother and I cried together for two days straight, I think, just sitting on the couch and eating something from time to time, but mostly crying. We drank a lot of tea together and then we calmed down. 'You have to leave,' she told me, 'look at what happened to your friends and classmates. People are being killed or disappearing. Even if you are far away in the U.S., at least I'll know where you are and that you're safe.' I knew she was right, but it was so painful to leave. My brother had died six months ago, her second child that died, and she was not the same after that. She never was the same again. I thought if I stayed, I could help, but if I was killed, I don't know what she would do. I didn't want to leave.

"My father was convinced Chile was heading in the right direction. He said he would use his connections with the new government to get me a job. I didn't believe him. He couldn't erase my past activism, and I couldn't swallow my beliefs. If that was the only way to stay in Chile, then I would rather leave.

"One of my last memories of Chile was going to the U.S. Embassy to get permission to go to the U.S. We had applied for my resident status, and now the officer began questioning me. Did I want to overthrow the government or conduct anti-government activities in the U.S.? That question has stayed with me all these years. Just months after aggressively intervening in my country's democracy and helping to overthrow our government, a U.S. official was asking me if I wanted to do the same to his country? And he had the power to keep me out of his country if I said yes!

"We flew to Los Angeles and I remember looking out the window of the plane and seeing the city below us. It was all concrete with lines and lines of cars and freeways wrapping around the city, like they were strangling it. There were huge buildings too. Now when I go to Los Angeles, I find it similar in some ways to Santiago. It's so spread out and wide and there's smog too. But back then Santiago wasn't the large capital of a thriving country, like it is today.

"From the airplane, everything below scared me and once we landed that fear only grew. The questions that had started at the embassy in Chile only grew fiercer. They started immediately: Why, why, why are you here? The questions seemed eternal. The official looked like a cop and under the dictatorship, cops and military were one and the same in Chile, so it was very triggering for me and I struggled to answer the questions. Scared is the only word I can use. That was how I felt the whole time. The paperwork was all there. But I felt like I was doing something wrong, like I was tricking the officer somehow, trying to enter his country without permission. Arriving without an invitation. The official treated me like I would be treated for my entire life in the U.S. They let me in eventually after so many questions because I had a visa. I had permission to enter the country, stamped by the U.S. embassy. I was legal.

"I remember walking out of the airport and seeing a surprise: the first street that I saw in the United States was Sepulveda Boulevard, just like my last name. It felt like a strange coincidence, and I took it as a welcome sign to my new home.

"Then I started to see all the people rushing around, like busy ants, rushing from here to there, to work, to work some more and then work again. They all looked like they were going to the same place, rushed, but because they were all rushed, it seemed like they were in rhythm. We walked around the streets and I saw the separation immediately. Latinos with Latinos and their own supermarkets, their own restaurants with food from their countries. African Americans with African Americans. Asians with their own spaces and their own stores, their own town within the city. White people with white people, in the nicest places with the prettiest houses. Nobody made eye contact on the streets; they were all in their own world. It felt lonely. For them and for me.

"The streets and cars were wild. The freeways—I loved that word as soon as I learned it. Everything in the U.S. was free or had the word free in it. Freedom. Land of the Free. Freeways. There was such pride in the concept of freedom, but it was also self-conscious, like an overcompensation even, so much so that I don't know if people knew what it meant anymore. There were dozens of white lines on the freeways and cars crossing them at will, free to move and go as fast as I've ever seen a car go. The cars made me dizzy. There were never families in the cars. It was always one or two people, going and going, never smiling.

"I thought I had gotten off the plane in the wrong city, in the wrong country. The Hollywood movies I had seen never had Latinos, African Americans, or Asians. Hollywood was a paradise made reality in my mind. A place where all the happy families lived. This didn't seem like the place.

"Some people that we knew took us to lunch. They thought I would want to eat food that I knew in case I was homesick. So we went to a Mexican restaurant and they ordered tacos and burritos. In Chile, tacos are the heels of shoes and burritos are little donkeys. Neither sounded very appetizing, but I didn't say anything. When the food came, it was actually pretty good.

"I'll never forget that day. I remember going to sleep thinking: Why did I come here? What am I doing here? I missed Chile and I missed my mother. We had never been this far from each other. There was nothing waiting for me in this new country, I thought.

"Not long after I arrived in the U.S., Richard Nixon resigned. They were going to impeach him if he didn't. At the time, it didn't seem important to me. I couldn't really read the newspapers because my English wasn't very good. I also didn't know how much Nixon had done to destabilize Chile, to bring Pinochet to power. That all came out years later. But looking back, it's strange to think that a man that was indirectly or even directly responsible for me leaving Chile was also forced to leave right when I arrived here. It has a nice poetic symmetry to it.

"After a year working at a restaurant, the restaurant owner's wife saw me crying one day after work and we talked after closing, late into the night. She was a kind woman and an alcoholic, who spent too much time at the bar in the restaurant. I told her I wanted to go back to school but didn't know how or if I could and I didn't know what I was doing here. She told me something that changed my life. She said: 'I'm going to bet on you.' She convinced her husband to create a scholarship for me under the condition that I keep a 3.6 or higher GPA and to give me shifts at the restaurant to fit school. Tuition wasn't as expensive as it is today, but it was still incredibly generous. Something like that would have never happened in Chile. I barely spoke English, but I bought a new tape recorder and memorized every lecture. I read books slowly, with a dictionary nearby that I used for every tenth word. I worked a lot at the restaurant still too. I don't remember sleeping much.

"That was the start. I haven't left the university since then. I don't know if it has been the American Dream. It was a nightmare in a lot of places, but it's better than what would've happened to me in Chile. I look back and it was so long ago that I don't feel like an immigrant. I'm made to feel like an immigrant often. Brown skin, accent . . . *Where are you from?* But I've lived twice as many years in the U.S. as I have in Chile. Two-thirds of my life here in the U.S. My God where has the time gone?

"Now, though, I feel that it's time for me to be back to Chile. After so many people telling me to 'go back where I came from' for so many years, I'm finally going to take their advice. But then I wonder, is it too late? When I left Chile, I thought that I would be back in a few months. I thought Pinochet and the military junta wouldn't last. I didn't say goodbye to anyone other than my mother. I didn't know where anyone else was, or if they were alive. I only took one backpack with me. My mother sent me boxes of things as the years passed and eventually there was nothing left of mine in Chile, and I began to wonder if there was nothing left of me, then, in Chile. The house we used to live in is still there, I've been to see it. But it felt like looking at a museum of my life: 'Here lived Emma Sepúlveda until 1974.' I keep thinking there is something back there for me, but maybe I don't belong anywhere. People drew the lines between countries and we have been lost ever since."

3

Immigration law today is not the same immigration law that my mother faced in 1974. Indeed, immigration law today has little in common with the 1965 Hart-Celler Act, which, on face value, did away with an outdated and racist quota system for new immigrant arrivals, opening American borders from a more Eurocentric system to a global purview that would include Africans, Asians, and Latin Americans. Riding in on the coattails and strength of the civil rights movement, it was signed by Lyndon Johnson as part of his Great Society reforms and remained the law when my mother arrived. Speaking from Liberty Island where the bill was signed, looking out onto the shores of New York City, President Johnson stressed that this new law would allow immigrants to come to the United States based on their skills and their familial ties so that no one would be "kept apart because a husband or a wife or a child had been born in the wrong place." He admonished the old immigration system and lauded the bill he would be signing, saying, "We can now believe that it [the old system] will never again shadow the gate to the American Nation with the twin barriers of prejudice and privilege."

The new law was imperfect, but President Johnson believed it would change the perception and administration of the previous laws that immigrants endured in arriving in the United States. His vice president, Hubert Humphrey, believed the same. "We have removed all elements of second-class citizenship from our laws by the [1964] Civil Rights Act," professed Humphrey. "We must in 1965 remove all elements in our immigration law which suggest there are second-class people."

Both Johnson and Humphrey were hopeful but naive. The intent of the law, while perhaps egalitarian in origin, overlooked its potential effects and as such, the unforeseen consequences were vast. The Hart-Celler Act, broadly speaking, created "illegal" immigration as we know it today and fundamentally altered the demographics of the United States, changing the face of America. This was not, of course, the intention. Instead, the Hart-Celler Act was focused on removing the codified nativism that was established with the 1924 Johnson-Reed Act. The 1924 law established the aforementioned quota-based system, which relied on national origins to determine eligibility to enter the United States. It fixed close to three-fourths of the immigrant visas to northern Europeans and drastically limited immigration from southern and eastern Europe. The bars on entry for immigrants from Asia and Africa from the turn of the century continued and, in fact, gained in strength in the Johnson-Reed Act. By removing this quota system, race was said to no longer factor into immigration.

And yet, on the final push before the 1965 Act was passed, a compromise was included to cap immigration from the Western Hemisphere for the first time. The numerical limit was set at 120,000—this was further limited in 1976 to basic caps of 20,000 a year on each nation in the Western Hemisphere, even though Mexicans seeking permanent residence in the United States had commonly surpassed 50,000 in the previous years. At the same time, in 1964, the Bracero Program, which had been in effect intermittently since 1942 and brought Mexican workers to the United States in a lawful program to work in U.S. agriculture in numbers exceeding 400,000 a year, ended. Ironically, it was discontinued as a liberal reform to reduce farmworker labor violations. The need for labor, however, and the higher rates of pay available in the United States compared to Latin America, continued. The numerical limits on immigration from Latin America were arbitrarily set and labor demands were not considered, despite a rapidly expanding agricultural sector and growing economy.

The population in Latin America expanded rapidly in the decades following 1965, and political and economic stability were rampant in the region, often because of U.S. covert and overt operations to protect "democracy" and business interests, like, for example, the copper mines in Chile that had been nationalized under President Allende. Additionally, because of the blowback from the Vietnam War and the continuing battle waged against Fidel Castro, the United States focused its refugee admissions on few places that assuaged public opinion and satisfied geopolitical concerns. It was not until the Refugee Act of 1980 that a uniform and comprehensive policy was created for asylum, where the geographic and supposed ideological limitation on the definition of "refugee" that had been introduced by the 1965 Act was removed and permanently reformed. The new law formally adopted the United Nations' definition of a refugee and set an annual number of refugee admissions, to be decided by the president in consultation with Congress. For this reason, people like my mother in 1974, had she not been married to a U.S. citizen, likely would not have been classified as a refugee or been eligible for asylum in the United States.

The Hart-Celler Act, by prioritizing family reunification, also created "chain migration," which refers to the manner in which immigrants sponsor family members to come to the United States based on their lawful permanent residency or citizenship. A recent example is First Lady Melania Trump sponsoring her parents to come to the United States, after which they were able to naturalize and become U.S. citizens. It has come under scrutiny lately, but almost immediately after the 1965 act went into effect, the family-based sponsorship process resulted in a much larger than expected number of applicants. Due to this, today lawful permanent residents and U.S. citizens in the United States who want to sponsor family members from China, India, and Mexico are likely looking at a twenty-year wait before a visa is available to their family members. When people speak about "waiting in line" to legally immigrate to the United States, this is what the line looks like, and the queue was first set up in the Hart-Celler Act.

While the United States moved through shifting policies and priorities with immigration, my mother was trying to get a handle on U.S. culture as a recent arrival. Because the majority of Spanish-speaking immigrants in the 1970s—and still today—were Mexican, my mother was often confused for Mexican. She spoke very little English, and to make matters more confusing, her first job in the United States, where she made just under $1 an hour, was as a hostess at a Mexican restaurant. When she told people that she was from Chile, the diners at the restaurant assumed that Chile was a city in Mexico or a Mexican spice to add to their tacos and burritos.

A year or so after she started working at the restaurant, she witnessed what so many have endured throughout the history of immigration enforcement: a workplace raid. While standing in the kitchen eating a quick meal of rice and beans before her shift began, she heard people shouting *La Migra! La Migra!* The noisy kitchen emptied in a flash, pans rattling and echoing on the heels of the dispersal. The cooks and dishwashers yelled over their shoulders at my mother: *Corre! Corre!* She took off her high heels and sprinted out the back door, close behind her co-workers. She had no idea what was happening; she did not know what *la Migra* meant. Yet coming from the military dictatorship in Chile, when someone told you to run, you ran for your life. She didn't know if it was a robbery or if she would hear bullets firing.

It wasn't until later, when she returned to the restaurant after some time, sweating and still barefoot, that the owner of the restaurant explained to her, in his limited Spanish, that she did not need to run from *la Migra* because she had a *tarjeta verde.* My mother still did not understand. She shook her head vigorously. *Yo no tengo tarjeta verde.* The only documentation that immigration had given her was a blue card that said *Resident*

Alien across the top in capitalized blue letters. The name for a permanent resident card had become fixed in everyone's mind, even though after 1976 the cards were no longer green in color and would not be again until 2010. When my mother became friends with a Mexican-American who was hired as the restaurant's second hostess, the situation was more clearly explained to her. She came to grasp that she was lawfully in the United States and as such, she did not need to run when *la Migra* conducted an immigration raid.

From this story, I learned something that I have seen repeatedly in my work as an immigrant advocate. While immigrants in general are treated differently in the United States, there is a hierarchy within this treatment as well, both within the legal system and society: those with documentation—certain visas, green cards, citizenship—occupy a different position than those without. They are privileged. Like my mother when the raid occurred, they do not have to fear in the same way—they are not keeping a secret that at any moment could be discovered and ruin their lives.

Shortly after witnessing the immigration raid, my mother gave up her Chilean citizenship and became a U.S. citizen. She was able to vote in an election for the first time, right as the presidential election of 1980 was arriving. She voted for Jimmy Carter and would later disagree with many of Reagan's policies, particularly in Central America, but she was struck deeply by the words he spoke during his inaugural address, the first time she heard a U.S. president speak as a U.S. citizen, and she felt he was speaking to her:

> *These visitors to that city on the Potomac do not come as white or black, red or yellow; they are not Jews or Christians; conservatives or liberals; or Democrats or Republi-*

cans. They are Americans awed by what has gone before,
proud of what for them is still . . . a shining city on a hill.

It was the same President Reagan who signed the Immigration Reform and Control Act (IRCA) in 1986, a carrot-and-stick bill that offered a path to lawful status for close to three million undocumented immigrants, while also increasing border security and creating penalties for employers who knowingly hired undocumented immigrants. The bill's sponsors called it the "three-legged stool" approach to immigration reform. IRCA is most known for the large-scale amnesty provisions, but in a lesser-known provision, it also marked the first time that federal funding was offered to states for the costs of incarcerating undocumented immigrants who had committed crimes, arguably offering a glimpse of what would become the criminal-immigration pipeline and vast business of immigrant detention.

4

I first visited Chile in 1991, when I was four years old. I remember the arrival more than anything else. We had left winter in the United States—there were several feet of snow in Nevada—and we were going to spend Christmas in Chile. I had on a thick jacket when we boarded the place. Twelve hours later, during which time I had mostly slept, we arrived in the early summer of Santiago, a heat no less humid and unbearable than the kind I would come to know in New York City. I awoke to the thick sunlight rising over the Andes. My four-year-old mind could not register the time passed, or the distance traveled. As we stepped off the plane, I realized I did not need my jacket. It was, in fact, extremely warm. I had never known a Christmas without snow, let alone with summer weather. We were in Santiago's then newly built airport, which was bustling with people. Outside the large glass windows, I saw the Andes for the first time. I don't remember much else, not the relatives we visited or the places we were taken to, but I do remember the weather and the landscape, easy stimulations for a child to take in. What I didn't realize was that my mother had returned for the first time to Chile as a democratic nation. I looked at my mother and yelled "It's a miracle!" She replied "Yes, it is." I could see that she was tearing up, and I assumed that she must have been as excited about the novelty of an exotic Christmas as I was. Only now do I know what those tears really meant.

In 1988, instead of a general election, a national plebiscite had taken place in Chile. Chileans were given two votes for one candidate: Voting *Yes* meant that General Pinochet would remain in power for another eight years, continuing and legitimizing his despotic rule. *No* was a rejection of the candidate (Pinochet). The plebiscite had been hatched in 1980, when a new constitution was created and approved through fraudulent means. The constitution called for a transition period—eight years long—wherein the Pinochet-led military junta would continue in power, until a candidate would be put forth to the voters in 1988. Pinochet, unwilling to relinquish power, imposed himself as the candidate and was particularly confident that he would win—that *Yes* would be the decision of a majority of Chileans.

Through brilliant marketing and overwhelming courage, the *No* campaign was victorious. The shock of *No* winning turned to anger within the Pinochet regime, and without overwhelming international and big business pressure to accept the results, Pinochet may have remained in power in spite of the vote. When I stepped onto Chilean soil as a four-year-old holding my mother's hand, Patricio Aylwin was president, the first democratically elected president since Salvador Allende in 1970, and ironically, as senator and president of the Christian Democratic Party in the late 1960s and early '70s, a staunch opponent of Allende's during his short-lived and tumultuous presidency. Pinochet, however, did not go away quietly: he became a senator for life and the fifty-plus amendments that were added to the 1980 constitution in 1990 after the transition to democracy had his fingerprints all over them. He towered over Chile then and, in countless ways (since many of those amendments remain in effect today) still does.

I didn't know any of this at the time. The only thing I knew about Chile was that it was the place that took my mother away from me for several weeks every so often. During the last decade, my mother and a colleague began working with the *arpilleristas*, women who were wives, daughters, and sisters of the "disappeared"—those that the Pinochet regime had taken away from their families and from whom nothing was ever heard again. The *arpilleristas* used needles and cloth as their resistance: mostly working-class homemakers, their sewing skills allowed them to create protest art depicting the repression in Chile. The woven patchworks they created sometimes used scraps of clothing from their "disappeared" family members when they could not obtain other materials. The scenes in the patchwork tapestries (*arpilleras*, as they are called) began asking questions about their "disappeared" family members: *Where are they? Why were they taken?* They sought answers, but as the years passed, they also sought the remains of family members that they knew were likely dead—a final answer, something akin to closure, as they searched morgues and jails for their loved ones.

As the 1980s progressed, while never giving up on their family members, they began fighting for democracy by depicting everyday struggles. The Pinochet regime operated with strict censorship but viewed the *arpilleristas* as a minimal threat, largely because they were women and they believed they could not be toppled or threatened by the protests of women. My mother and her colleague believed differently. For years, they risked their lives traveling to Chile and meeting with the *arpilleristas*, eventually stowing hundreds of *arpilleras* in their suitcases at the behest of their makers so that the world could know their stories and see their art. My mother, having given up her Chilean citizenship and traveling with an American passport, managed to escape notice on her travels. Taking this risk was also a small absolution of the guilt she felt in having avoided the experience that so many *arpilleristas* had gone through. Yet their stories and nonviolent protest inspired my mother, galvanizing her toward the biggest political act of her life

5

One of my favorite family artifacts is a televised campaign ad from 1994. It's only thirty seconds long, but opens with and is narrated by Senator Harry Reid, years before he became the Democratic and later majority leader of the Senate. "Hi, I'm Harry Reid," he begins. "One person running for office this year is truly committed to making our community a place to live. That person is Emma Sepúlveda." Reid was advocating for my mother's run for Nevada's state senate as a Democrat in 1994, itself a challenge to her district's incumbent Republican state senator who had run unopposed for nearly a decade. In doing so, she became the first Latina senatorial candidate in the state's history and a voice for immigrant rights. The timing wasn't coincidental: at the time, California was getting ready to pass Proposition 187—also known as Save Our State, or S.O.S.—to severely limit access to most public benefits, including education, for undocumented immigrants and establish a statewide citizenship screening program in the aftermath of economic recession nationwide. As a quarter of Nevada is Latino, the fear that such a proposal would leak into the Nevada legislation made her platform prescient.

My mother decided that she would walk, door-to-door, to every house in our district, knocking on doors and reaching out to all the nearly thirty thousand registered voters in the district in this manner. On several occasions, I accompanied her with my sister, though this did not last for very long. While canvassing, the divergence of opinion, and the ferociousness with which these opinions were expressed to my mother weren't just shocking to my sister and myself, but dangerous as well. On one occasion, a man shoved my mother and told her to *get the hell off my property and out of my country.* Another time, a man opened the door holding a shotgun after watching her walk up the path to his house from the window. After those run-ins, my mother decided two things: I would no longer canvas with her and she would avoid houses with NRA bumper stickers on the cars outside.

The Latino population, on the other hand, was uniformly friendly. *La candidata* was treated like royalty: they asked to take pictures with her, invited her to eat lunch with them in their homes. They usually gave me ice cream or a Popsicle, sometimes candy. They could not believe that a Latina candidate was running for office and wanting to represent them. But they were also apathetic: What would really change for them in this country by voting? Despite my mother's intent, she certainly faced an uphill battle both for the election and, if she won, from bigoted pushback. And it came when, during the campaign, a bill like Proposition 187 was proposed on the Senate floor. As one of its most vocal opponents, my mother showed the Latino community she was willing to fight for them, but that challenge came at a cost to her safety.

The things that I saw and heard while canvassing were amplified and, quite literally, brought home to us throughout the campaign. Whenever I was with her, words like *greaser* and *beaner* and *wetback* would be hurled our way. Because our number was listed in the phone book, people began leaving messages on our answering machine. At the time, I was going through a phase of sneaking up on people and scaring them. One evening, I tiptoed toward my mother's office, preparing to scare her with a *boo* or *surprise* as she listened to her messages. The sounds of the recorded voices masked my footsteps, but before I could surprise her, a heavy, breathy man's voice came on the answering machine. He started to speak in a harsh and loud voice, as if he were trying to send his words more forcefully through the receiver on his phone. *I'm going to kill you, you dirty . . . fucking . . . spick. You are going to dieeeee before I let you be my senator. Either go back to where you came from or I'll shoot you myself.* I walked into my mother's office, unable to scare her and continue with my prank. The man on the answering machine had scared us both. I stood completely still and looked at my mother. She looked back at me and didn't know what to say. It was even more terrifying because the voice I had heard before the man's was my own: my mother had recently enlisted me to record an automatic message for callers in English and Spanish, and so when anyone called, it was the voice of a child, and not hers, that apologized to them for her not being available.

In the weeks leading up to election night, I had come to yell back at the messages being left on the answering machine—I shouted at the voices *She's American!* as if that would make a difference, as if this were all a misunderstanding. I was greatly relieved when on the day of the election it was announced that the incumbent had won once again. I felt she was now safe from those people who were threatening her life. But even still, my mother stayed active in politics, forming and leading a nonprofit aimed at the political education and voter registration of the Latino population in Northern Nevada. She worked behind the scenes now, and I often tagged along to help those in the Latino community register to vote. Momentous changes to immigration law were unfolding, and even though Nevada's version of Proposition 187 was struck down (as was California's and all other states that tried to enact similar bills), many others would have lingering and prevailing effects.

6

Like they did in Chile and many other countries in Latin America, the United States once again moved to stymie the threat of a socialist-leaning government by sending millions of dollars to a right-wing military authority to prevent it. The Salvadoran Civil War was one of the biggest conflicts to take place in the Western Hemisphere during the last quarter of the twentieth century. And as happens with conflict, thousands of Salvadorans migrated north to the United States hoping for refuge in its aftermath. Among them was a fifteen-year-old girl by the name of Jenny Flores, who was detained at the U.S. border. The Immigration and Naturalization Service (the precursor to ICE) would continue to detain her and would not release her to anyone but a parent—though if such a parent were also undocumented, he or she could be deported too—and thus parents, like Jenny's mother, out of fear, did not go pick up their children. Carlos Holguín, a lawyer in Los Angeles, received a phone call from a Hollywood actor whose housekeeper was Jenny Flores's mother. He explained that INS was holding Jenny at a makeshift detention center. When Holguin arrived, he saw a dilapidated 1950s motel, recently cleared of prostitutes and drug addicts, surrounded by a chain-link fence and concertina wire, like a concentration camp in the middle of the Hollywood neighborhood of Los Angeles. The swimming pool on the property had been drained. Adults and children of both sexes mingled freely on the property. They were housed at least four people to a room. There was no school and nothing to do. Everyone was just being held there, with no concern for safety or livable conditions. Everyone was strip-searched regularly, separated by just a screen from those of the opposite sex. Jenny's father had been killed in El Salvador. Holguin and other attorneys filed a class-action lawsuit, which, after working its way up to the Supreme Court, eventually resulted in the *Flores* Settlement Agreement in 1997, agreed to by the Clinton administration and its attorney general, Janet Reno.

The *Flores* Settlement Agreement established basic protections for immigrant youth, including the parameters of their release to sponsors, the treatment they are required to receive while detained, and the conditions of their confinement, so that no immigrant youth would ever have to go through what Jenny Flores once went through. Through subsequent litigation, the courts have decided that the *Flores* Settlement Agreement applies equally to unaccompanied and accompanied minors—meaning that immigrant youth that arrive with their parent(s) are allotted the same protections and must be released from detention within twenty days if they are detained in a facility that is not licensed to hold children. To this day, litigation on the *Flores* Settlement Agreement is ongoing, for the most part because both the Obama administration and the Trump administration—

especially—have failed to meet its requirements in their treatment of immigrant youth, yet it remains a pivotal and landmark instrument to protect one of the most vulnerable populations.

Meanwhile, as negotiations on the *Flores* Settlement Agreement were drawing to a close, Newt Gingrich and the Republican Party were signing a Contract with America. The Clinton administration—not unlike the Obama administration a decade later—wanted to show they were tough on crime and immigration, and so they signed on as well. The results included the Illegal Immigration Reform and Immigrant Responsibility Act (IIRIRA) and the Antiterrorism and Effective Death Penalty Act, both passed in 1996. Each altered pointedly the immigration enforcement landscape, but it was IIRIRA that made abundant and sweeping changes to U.S. immigration laws, fathering the current deportation apparatus and orphaning any semblance of humanity in the laws.

IIRIRA included a significantly expanded range of criminal convictions for which legal permanent residents could be automatically deported, especially minor and nonviolent offenses, while also making it much more difficult for people fleeing persecution to apply for asylum. The act further eradicated important deportation defenses and endangered many more immigrants, including legal permanent residents, to detention and deportation. IIRIRA likewise increased enforcement and streamlined deportation proceedings along the border and within 100 miles of the border, paving the way for the border situation we see today. Finally, IIRIRA created the three- and ten-year bars: if someone accrued six months or more of unlawful status in the United States, they would be barred from reentering for three years if they were to leave the country; if someone accrued over a year of unlawful presence, they would trigger a ten-year bar upon leaving and attempting to reenter. This meant that nearly all undocumented immigrants began staying in the United States perpetually, increasing the total undocumented population, and that most—who were not eligible for a waiver of the bars—were now unable to adjust their status to that of lawful permanent resident since such adjustment required leaving the United States, thus trapping those in the United States in a continually undocumented status. Whereas focus has shifted to more recent policies affecting immigrants, we dismiss any of this history at our own peril: the immigration war of today is being fought with weapons loaded by IIRIRA and shields first forged by the *Flores* Settlement Agreement. Though I was clueless to many of these battles, for my mother these were monumental fights, but the battleground was about to change.

7

For my mother, September 11 will forever be a date that marked two tragedies—the day Pinochet took power in Chile in 1973, and the day, almost thirty years later, when the twin towers of the World Trade Center fell, and the entire world as we knew it forever changed. At fourteen, it was a world I was barely conscious of. People had crowded into a middle-school mathematics classroom where our teacher, Mr. Vaughn, had a television turned on silent to the news. We watched as the smoke billowed out from the upper floors, and cuts of the planes crashing into them were replayed. Mr. Vaughn, nervously cracked an inappropriate joke. *Those terrorists must have a sense of humor if they did this on 9-1-1. Get it? Like you call 9-1-1 when there's an emergency?* Rather than being callous, it was likely he didn't know what else to say—no one did, not even the counselors who were forced to shuffle through our fluorescent-lit classrooms to speak with us. My mother picked me up from school that day trembling with fear. So many things, down to the date, repeated itself that morning.

Like most people, I can recall the events of 9/11 with uncanny precision, and through the subsequent Bush years and his war on terror, perhaps the scariest time for anyone in America who didn't have white skin, I had an awakening as a politically active citizen. But even after college, I wasn't quite sure what it was that I wanted to do with my life. And so, at the encouragement of my mother, I left the United States for a solo trip to Chile and throughout Latin America. I thought that I would find meaning with a backpack strapped on and a couple of notebooks and camera to document it all. I read Kerouac religiously and had vague ideas about human rights. My thoughts, however, solidified and came into focus after two events.

For the first time, I spent September 11 outside of the United States. My mother's relationship to the Chilean 9/11 didn't really have significance for me until, upon arriving and wanting to do something other than see the sights, I reached out to a group of protestors who were opposed to the possible return of a conservative presidential administration. It was the anniversary of the military coup, and after electing the country's first female president in 2006, the country was shifting to the right and threatening to elect the first conservative president since the return to democracy in 1990. A younger generation of voters, who had grown up only knowing democracy, were careless with their votes and their voices.

The group invited me to a march to the *Estadio Nacional*, Chile's national soccer stadium where more than twenty thousand men and women were kept, many tortured and some killed, during the early days of the military junta. One month later, I would return to the stadium and watch the Chilean national team beat the Argentine national team 1–0 in a shocking victory. The stadium would be crowded, full of rabid fans, agonizing for ninety minutes until the stadium erupted in euphoria. All except the wooden benches behind the north goal, where no one has sat for years, a permanent memorial to the atrocities that took place within the stadium. But on that night, as we marched with signs and flashlights and candles, the stadium was eerily empty. I heard speeches detailing the horrors that took place within the stadium's walls. One man that survived being tortured there spoke movingly about the need for dignity and respect for all human life. *Estamos aquí juntos en esta vida, no para hacernos daño, pero para cuidarnos.*

Six months later, I was living in a studio in Sucre, Bolivia, teaching English and working part time at an orphanage. One afternoon, I heard that President Evo Morales would be visiting Sucre, in celebration of the anniversary of the first *Grito Libertario*, announcing the revolutionary independence movement from Spain. The main square of Sucre, like always, was packed with indigenous men and women peddling coca leaves and their handmade wares. Soon, they would be going to the *Estadio Olímpico Patria*, Bolivia's most important sports facility, capable of holding more than thirty thousand people, to see the first indigenous president in the nearly two-hundred-year history of Bolivia speak. They walked and chanted in Quechua. They handed out coca leaves to those of us walking with them. I stuffed a wad of leaves into my left cheek after an indigenous man showed me how. I pulled out my camera and snapped a photo of the proud faces I saw among the crowd, finally represented by one of their own. Suddenly, an angry mob of anti-Morales people armed with thick sticks charged into the crowd. Nearby, police were attacked as well. The government, hearing about these disturbances hours before Morales's speech, canceled all scheduled parades and the president's visit. Once the police and military presence was gone, the indigenous men and women who had come to see the president were left alone with armed civilians from urban and wealthy Sucre, the same people that had oppressed them for decades, now unable to accept an awakened and powerful indigenous population. More than two dozen indigenous men and women were injured. I stood there for a moment and watched the scene unfold through the lens of my camera, unable to look away and not taking any more photos. I may as well have been watching the news on television. A man held up a stick like a baseball bat, threatening me and yelling at me in Spanish to put my camera away and leave. I rushed back to the studio I was renting and tried to write it all down. I wrote three pages, my hand shaking, and found myself disappointed. What would I do with these pages? I imagined myself being able to freeze time and space and take the indigenous men and women to safety, leaving their tormentors bewildered when unfrozen. That was what I really wanted to do.

When I thought about it, though, I knew that there would never be a way to freeze time or to protect anyone from such a sudden, unprovoked attack. But perhaps there was a way to go back in time. Instead of taking someone out of harm's way, I could help them return to that place, protected, and seek redress and justice for what they had suffered. And in doing so, we could affect the future, eliminating the possibility of that occurring again. The next week, armed with memories from the march to Chile's *Estadio Nacional* and what I had seen in Sucre, I signed up for the LSAT and began gathering the documents needed to apply to law school.

During my first year of law school, I realized I was there because of my mother. The things I had seen her do throughout the years were hidden seeds that I felt were finally receiving the nourishment they deserved. She was inspiration and consciousness for me. The simultaneous love for and questioning of America came from her, as did the exploration of being the "other." She wanted the country to be better and yet defended it fiercely.

I applied for summer jobs at legal aid and nonprofit organizations around California. That seemed like the front lines, and that was where I wanted to be. I came across a summer position in Watsonville at the Watsonville Law Center and was offered the position on the spot. I'd never been to Watsonville. I had to look on a map. When I saw that it was close to Santa Cruz, I jumped at the opportunity. I found a fellowship that would give me a small amount of money to do the work I would be doing, and then I found a couple who rented me a cheap room in exchange for doing their yard work.

Two weeks into the job, I met a female farmworker who made everything real and helped me decide that this was what I wanted to do. She stopped by one of our weekly clinics at six o'clock. She was from Chiapas, Mexico, where the Zapatista movement began. For three hours I sat with her as she told me all the things that she had never told anyone. She was alone here. Her two kids had stayed in Mexico with her mother; she had given birth to three kids, but her youngest daughter had died. Her father was dead. Her husband had run off with another woman to Southern California. Good riddance, he used to beat her. Some of the workers on the farm where she worked were sexually abusing her. She had gotten pregnant and miscarried. She told me this as if it were her fault. When she stopped talking, I tried to find a way to help. I was new to the work, but I had been trained to look for a few things. She was getting paid far below the minimum wage and working eighty hours a week with no overtime. California in those days, like other states, had

different laws for farmworkers. They would not get paid overtime until they had worked ten hours in a day and sixty hours
in a week, as opposed to eight and forty for most other jobs. As
for pay, even undocumented immigrants are afforded the protections of minimum wage. She didn't know what overtime meant,
or that there was a minimum wage. I tried to explain both with
my still evolving understanding of each.

By the end of the month, we had filed a wage and hour complaint and were scheduled to appear at the Labor Commissioner's office in Salinas. I talked with the woman about filing an
OSHA complaint or looking for ways to improve her working
conditions with regards to the sexual abuse, but she said no. She
was Catholic and a married woman still, and she did not want to
talk about the things that had happened to her in the fields anymore to anyone, just God. When we arrived at the Labor Commissioner's office in Salinas, ready for an administrative hearing,
we found a check for ten thousand dollars waiting for us. After
doing the math, my supervisor and I had only been prepared to
ask for seven thousand. The woman was shocked. She looked at
us like we were saints, when we had only used a spreadsheet to
make calculations and submitted a form.

The next day, the woman arrived at our office with two
baskets of freshly picked strawberries and a handwritten note.
*Nunca me han ayudado en la vida y nunca pensé que me iba a
ayudar nadie. Que Dios le bendiga.* She left them at the front
desk, and I never got to speak with her and I never saw her
again. She might still be working in the fields. Maybe she finally
sent for her children with the money she received. Maybe she
left and went back to Chiapas. But no matter where I am, even if
the strawberries are not from Watsonville, I am still reminded of
her when I bite into one. There was justice, imperfect as it might
be, I told myself. The law was a weapon, and, in some cases, it

could be wielded for the benefit of communities it was written to oppress.

The summer went on like this, with dozens of farmworkers coming in every week. One man went to a *curandero* because he was not feeling well, and the *curandero* told him he was very ill and would die by the end of the year. For five thousand dollars in cash, he could cure him. The ointment he was given gave him such bad diarrhea that he had to go to a hospital, where a doctor told him he was perfectly healthy, other than dehydration from the diarrhea. The *curandero* had left town, and no one knew his name. The cash was gone. Another woman was getting paid two hundred dollars a week to wash dishes at a restaurant fulltime and when she asked for a raise, the owner threatened to call ICE. It had been my favorite restaurant in Watsonville, and the owner had brought me a free beer once with my tacos, but I stopped going. Other cases, I quickly saw, had no justice. The law was blunted in many ways, an instrument of the oppressor.

I started driving through the fields every morning before going to work. I would see the men and women in boots and bandannas, hunched over the infinite rows of strawberries and tomatoes. The sun was barely visible over the mountains, but they would already have picked hundreds of buckets full of the fruit or vegetable and dumped them into the trucks, which moved glacially with the workers from row to row. I started to think about the plates of food put in front of me in a restaurant. I would grab a raspberry in a grocery store and try to imagine the brown hands that had picked it. I would think of the people I had met and wonder if maybe one of them was responsible for this food arriving here. Every case that summer had a human story, and I needed to learn those stories and embrace them— that was the only way to do this work, I concluded. People, not cases. Even though, as I would learn years later, if you give every person that you represent a piece of your heart, there is little left for anyone else.

When I went back to start my second year of law school, I understood, finally, what I was studying for. Every class I took, I would look for ways to advocate for immigrants, to bend the law in favor of those it oppressed or forgot. I joined the Immigration Law Clinic and found life-changing mentors. I took an immigration law class. I learned about the Immigration and Nationality Act and read the various statutes it includes. I struggled to decipher the ways in which the different sections interacted with one another. Laws had been passed and others never repealed. The statute needed its own map. It felt like driving the roads in the South every time I opened the book: I could never get to where I wanted to go. But slowly, I began to discern meaning and learn the language. By the end of the semester, the INA was somewhat more accessible, and the vagueness of the language offered opportunities for creativity.

Before law school ended, though, I already had to put what I had learned into practice. I was tasked with the first immigration case that I would handle entirely on my own, even though I wasn't a lawyer yet. Alejandra, my wife, had been in the United States on a student visa that was set to expire soon after she graduated, and now that we were married, she could adjust her status to that of a lawful permanent resident based on her marriage to a U.S. citizen. I diligently read through all the instructions, collected the requisite evidence, and filled out the necessary paperwork. This was my first case, but it was also the most important, or the most personal at least—this was our life and we wanted to be together in the United States. Granted, we did not have as much to lose as some of the clients I had seen my mentors take on in the Immigration Law Clinic, people that would be killed in their home countries if their cases were not successful. But still I felt the pressure while compiling the application packet. Everyone has something to lose, and the privilege of carrying part of this burden is something I vowed not to forget as I started out as an immigration lawyer. And it was this thought, this personal approach and consideration of the consequences, that I would take with me into the subsequent cases that I worked on.

Six months later, soon after we had arrived in New York City and just a few weeks after Chloe was born, we received an interview notice. Alejandra and I would have to go to 26 Federal Plaza and sit for an interview with an immigration officer. In 1986, the Immigration Marriage Fraud Amendments began requiring petitioners to show that their marriage was "bona fide" and even when granted, people like Alejandra who had not been married to a U.S. citizen for more than two years would not immediately become lawful permanent residents. Instead, they would have "conditional" green cards for two years, during which time USCIS could further investigate. After two years, the couple would have to apply to have the conditions removed, at which time they would again need to show that they had a bona fide marriage that had continued since they were first approved.

A bona fide marriage for the purposes of immigration is shown not through deep commitment and true love, which admittedly are hard to provide physical evidence of, but through documentation. Marriages need paper trails for USCIS to believe that they are not fraudulent. And even then, as we would learn, there is a presumption of fraud that the petitioners must overcome.

Alejandra and I came armed with our lease agreement signed by both of us, our joint bank account, our wedding certificate, and two declarations from friends who had attended our wedding. It wasn't a lot of documentation, but we also came with the biggest, most irrefutable evidence: Chloe's birth certificate, where we were listed as the parents. Having a child for the purpose of securing evidence of a bona fide marriage seemed like something out of a Don DeLillo novel—no officer would take that stance. We were wrong on that account, or at least the USCIS officer made us feel that way. Even with the evidence we presented, the officer tore our marriage to bits, seeking out a fraud that was not there. Alejandra, quite nervous and used to the metric system, was unable to tell the officer my height, to which he replied, *Jesus, how can you not know that about your supposed husband?* After the interview, Alejandra left the building wiping tears from her eyes. I looked for ways to console her. I couldn't be sure if she was upset at the treatment of our marriage or if she thought we would be denied. Both, she told me. We sat on the train silently on the way home.

On a quiet, unassuming day soon thereafter, we received Alejandra's green card. The words on the letter that came with the green card said: "Welcome to the United States of America." They were the same confusing words that I would come to see many times later when I had successful outcomes on certain cases. Alejandra, like many of the immigrants I worked with, had already been in the United States for several years. The letter was a striking acknowledgment that they had been largely invisible before; only now was the United States welcoming them into its sacred fraternity. *Where was I before? Where have I been living for the last four years?* Alejandra asked. However much it stung Alejandra to see those words and remember the interview we had done, it was a vast improvement over and paled in comparison to the treatment that I would see along the border. There is no one welcoming anyone along the border.

It was not until we moved to Brooklyn and I began working for my organization that the full weight of 9/11 came into view. From where I sat in my office, I could see the Freedom Tower, the building often reflecting in the evening sun. It was a memorial, but also a glass peacock of patriotism, built taller than the buildings that stood there before. Delia and Wilson were two clients from Haiti who took strength from looking out my office window at the buildings of New York City, especially the Freedom Tower. They were just two years old when 9/11 happened. New York City didn't exist for them; the United States didn't either. They had no television or radio, no way of knowing that 1,500 miles north of their island of Hispaniola, another island, another country, would change forever—and as such, the world would too. Immigration would face abrupt and lasting changes following that day. Nine years later, the earth shook violently beneath Delia and Wilson's feet, and their home and their city disappeared around them. The ground continued to shake intermittently for days afterward, the rest of the remaining structures buckling to the ground, as if God were getting the crumbs off his carpet. They couldn't find their parents for a week, and everything they weren't wearing was lost or looted. They went to school, rain or shine, in a tent for more than a year after that. Everything they had ever known was reduced to rubble. They would leave their island for another, the one I saw in Mr. Vaughn's classroom, three tortuous years later. That a building could stand that tall and be rebuilt to such proportions seemed impossible after the devastation they had witnessed. It was perhaps why they both wanted to be architects, if not to help rebuild Haiti, then to build something strong, something lasting, the same thing that we all want. Their hope finally shown the first positive light on the long dark date of 9/11.

Change had come for my mother too, who, late in her life, finally followed her dream of returning to Chile, to returning *home*. I was happy for her, but surprised when she wrote me a long letter saying how she felt like a foreigner in Chile. What followed was her long sought out answer to the question of what home was supposed to mean:

It's like I'm from somewhere else now that I'm here and the same thing has always happened in the U.S. And that means I don't know who I am in one aspect, but it's also liberating because I do whatever the hell I want and don't try to be Chilean or American or anything anymore. Maybe old age is part of it. But there are no more expectations. There are no more homes. There is just my life, what's left of it at least, and how I want to live it. And where I want to live it.

PART III

THE BORDER

. . . .

Between the wish and the thing the world lies
waiting.

—*Cormac McCarthy*, All the Pretty Horses

Saturday, First Week

I have two equally powerful visions of the border—one fiction, one fact.

One is of the borderland—the barren, arid territory described poetically in the books of Cormac McCarthy. Its flora and fauna, its light and darkness, a land reduced to a strip between two worlds—McCarthy renders it in vivid detail and unforgiving prose. Intertwined with the reality of the immigrant, it becomes a space that is, as McCarthy writes, "undifferentiated in its terrain from the country they quit, yet wholly alien and wholly strange."

Which brings me to the obstacle: the border as a definitive boundary that many people, including the youths I work with, must cross, a before-and-after in their lives. I have heard their descriptions of it, their paths to it, their disappointments and triumphs after crossing it, and how it is also insurmountable, despite being, in most places, a line in the sand, or a rushing river. They were immigrants and my clients entirely because of this border, whether they were stopped crossing it or passed through it invisibly. To hear them tell it, the border was a harsh place, where nature is brutal, where people disappeared trying to cross it, and where men and women armed with enough fire-power and conviction to halt an army guarded it. Yet without a border there wouldn't be much to separate "us" from "them." While the length of the border spans nearly two thousand miles, it's width by comparison is measured in inches and feet, barely thick enough to be called an international division at all.

I had crossed over the border many times, mostly to visit Chile, but always by plane, never by foot. That would change near the beginning of 2016, when the Immigrant Justice Corps Fellowship I was on in New York City told the twenty-five lawyers and ten community fellows that we would all have the opportunity to work in two-week rotations with immigrants being held at detention centers along the U.S.–Mexico border. They wanted to expand their impact, and our small army of advocates was elated to participate. Our rotations were staggered so a new arrival could spend a week with a veteran to get acquainted. Funded by a New York–based hedge fund manager, the two-week rotation was entirely paid for. But this was no vacation, and while a free apartment was nice, I most welcomed the comfort of being able to have a place to digest the weight of what I was there to do.

I arrived in San Antonio via Charlotte, after sleeping the entire three hours of each of my two flights. This was my first time away from home since our daughter, Chloe, was born, and I stayed up watching her instead of preparing for the trip I was about to take. Chloe was only five months old, far too young to realize I'd be gone, or that's what I hoped at least. Though she wouldn't remember this, I wondered about the impact of my absence upon her. My wife, Alejandra, supported me in taking this journey, but now that the time to leave was upon us, I could sense a bit of frustration. She had paused her career to stay at home with Chloe, and though she felt a terrible guilt about leaving the house, she also wanted badly to resume work. She had been looking for jobs, but without me there, it would be difficult for her to go in for an interview. She'd have to wait until I came back.

Once I landed in the San Antonio airport, however, I had to push my own guilt out of my head to get into the mind of what I was there to do. At first glance, the setup seemed pretty cushy. The Chevy Equinox I would be driving was prepaid and was used by a previous fellow who had dropped it off earlier that morning before flying back home. We were lodged in an extended-stay apartment complex in the heart of Southtown, one of San Antonio's burgeoning hip and artsy neighborhoods. I arrived just as a woman was finishing cleaning my apartment, easily one of the nicest places I would ever stay in, with a complete kitchen, washer and dryer, a modern AC unit, and two TVs. Leena, as she introduced herself, was in her late thirties, maybe early forties, and had her small, tight curls of bleached blond hair pulled into a ponytail, a black bandanna keeping her forehead dry of sweat. She was friendly but complained about the little amount of time she had between fellows to get everything organized, despite the apartment being immaculate from where I stood. There was a knock at the open door and a young man, with a long handsome face and untraceable features, waved and entered the apartment. "Kennji," he said extending his hand. "I was just stepping out to grab a bite, care to join?" Leena looked relieved to hear me accept.

Kennji had been here a week and knew the layout of the neighborhood. I asked him if there was a good BBQ joint nearby. He told me that there was one within walking distance—a luxury in cities that lack public rapid-transit systems. Only later did he inform me that he was a vegetarian. "I didn't want to deny a new arrival a welcome barbeque," he said by way of explanation. It was the type of selfless gesture that in our week together I would come to know well from Kennji. I was all too happy to have the company and recommendation and followed his lead, taking in my surroundings with more bewilderment than the usual tourist. Though Texas reminded me of my home state of Nevada, San Antonio couldn't be farther from my Brooklyn home. Nearly equidistant from Los Angeles and Savannah and only a couple of hours from the Mexican border, the city was a crossroad of influences, where the Deep South seemed to drift into a Hollywood-esque Wild West. Lining the streets were towering palm trees and massive oaks draped with Spanish moss. Sleek modern architecture rubbed shoulders with old Franciscan missions and ivy-covered antebellum homes. Passing on the sidewalks were strollers and skateboarders, while gas-guzzling vehicles paraded by us on the adjacent multilane street.

On the outside, the BBQ joint resembled a saloon, but inside it turned out to be something straight out of Brooklyn: dozens of obscure beers, recycled furniture, small portions, and heavy prices. Nor did it serve traditional BBQ but *barbacoa*, a Mexican variation. It was rammed with a Saturday crowd—fit people with neck and sleeve tattoos and obese people wearing their Sunday best. Kennji and I had to wait nearly fifteen minutes to be seated. My ears perked up at the amount of Spanish I was hearing. Our waiter appeared to be of Mexican descent, as were several patrons. The menu was bilingual, and mariachi music emitted from the radio. I ordered ribs smothered in a mole sauce and washed it down with a bottle of Sol. More than anything, it seemed that San Antonio was a city that was inextricably interwoven with a Mexican heritage, as if a gust of wind had carried the dusty history of northern Mexico and spread it over the city.

As we ate, Kennji told me a bit about his work as a Manhattan-based asylum specialist, and I described my SIJS work out in Brooklyn. Because we worked in the same city, it was easy to break the ice by talking about our most and least favorite immigration judges, as well as the annoying security guard at 26 Fed who made everyone, even lawyers with passes, go through a security check. We got to talking about partners and families, and eventually came to discuss our own identities as children of immigrants, and what impact having a Chilean mother as I did, and having a Japanese father as he did, had on our lives.

Our food arrived, and Kennji switched the conversation to bring me up to speed on what to expect tomorrow morning. We would be traveling, he said. None of the facilities were in San Antonio, but much farther south, including the main facility we would be working from, the Karnes City Residential Center. "That's a misnomer," said Kennji. "It's a detention facility made to sound like a YMCA." He took a bite of his onion rings. I waited for him to swallow his bite, already forming a mental picture of the facility. "You're going to see things that will make you upset," he said looking up at me, hinting at my wife and daughter that we just spoke about, since we would be working exclusively with mothers and children at Karnes. "This is a whole new level, where undocumented women and children are held in a detention facility that once imprisoned single adult males. Now they're calling it a "family" center, with over two hundred families detained there, including close to three hundred children." He paused for a moment and forked some crumbs that had fallen from his veggie burger. "It's not even licensed to hold children," he said, still stabbing his plate, "and even the playground they installed can't change that."

Sunday, First Week

Kennji and I were up early for the hour-long drive south to Karnes City. The previous night, I had packed a few files and transfer memos left behind by the previous fellow, along with a lunch made with whatever I could find in the fridge, also left behind by the previous fellow. While at first I found it frivolous, it ended up making sense for each fellow to have his or her own transportation. Because each fellow took on different cases, schedules varied greatly: one fellow might need to stay in Karnes at the facility longer than the other, or might need to remain in San Antonio for an appearance at the immigration court. The offices of the Refugee and Immigrant Center for Education and Legal Services (RAICES), a Texas-based nonprofit, was the local point of contact for the fellows on rotation. It provided free and low-cost legal services, offered social support and education to the local communities, and was an invaluable resource in providing fellows with aid and research.

There wasn't much to see on Highway 181. The landscape was flat and grayish green. There were trees, but many of them seemed dead: thousands of stony trunks and branches buttressing various bushes for sunlight and space. Every now and then, however, a beautiful, wide, live oak would appear, sprinkled with moss that hung from crinkly branches that went off in every direction like an old spider on its back. Aside from the local flora were the sunburnt towns that the highway sometimes passed through. The smaller they were, the more dilapidated their buildings and homes. Trailer parks, uninhabited restaurants, and hair salons were the most common features, those and local high school pride. Nowhere was this more apparent than in Falls City. The town welcomed visitors with two signs, a small one stating its modest population of 611, and one seemingly ten times bigger, proudly proclaiming the Falls City Beavers high school football team as the 2010 Division 2 Class 1A state champions. I passed a Busy Beaver convenience store and a house with a large flag that read GO BEAVERS! Then it was gone; Beaver territory ended as abruptly as it started, at the city limits.

Karnes City was only another ten minutes farther, and as we came upon its city limits I noticed an abundance of big steel, khaki-colored oil drills. Their slow-moving, oblong-shaped heads gave the impression of massive praying mantises digging into the veins of the earth in order to remove its liquid gold. There was nothing around them but a short fence and the flat, dust-riddled land. I would find out later that Karnes City and the surrounding areas were intensive fracking sites and, as such, the water used in the Residential and Correctional Centers was heavily chlorinated, causing health issues for the immigrants detained within them.

Finally, we reached the city limits of Karnes City, two hours northeast of Laredo, the closest border point. Kennji flipped his blinker in a direction away from a sign that pointed toward the city center and toward a road bounded by a couple of buildings and cow pastures. Taking a glance in the direction of town, I could see a dusty street where the passing of a tumbleweed seemed more likely than anything that could be called a city. We had barely turned when Kennji immediately flicked the lights again, this time to the left toward two buildings and into a parking lot half-full of cars. "Welcome to the worst family vacation destination of all time," said Kennji.

We stepped out of our cars and very quickly, a strange feeling crept over me that I'd been here before. "This looks like the elementary and middle schools that I went to," I told Kennji. He turned his head in their direction and nodded his head. "They've cleverly made it look like that from the outside," he said. "The one that looks like an elementary school is the "Residential Center, which is for all woman and any children under 18, and the one next to it is the Karnes Correctional Center," said Kennji, "for any males 18 years of age or older." The subtle difference between "Residential" and "Correctional" belied the similarities between the two, which led me to wonder what the Correctional Center was trying to correct that the Residential Center was not. Being an immigrant in the United States seemed immutable, but perhaps there was some type of conversion therapy occurring within those walls.

The two buildings that made up the Karnes detention center were so nondescript that had I not followed Kennji into the parking lot, I could have easily driven past them, continuing into the undulating cow pastures. The Residential Center was a single-story khaki-colored building, thickly constructed so that its façade resembled a fortress, though someone had thought to give it a couple homely touches: its entrance was decorated with stucco portico painted a light blue and roofed with Spanish tiles. The Correctional Center also had a blue entrance, but bright, like the blue you'd find on an IKEA storefront. At both centers were equally blue benches shaded by awnings and accompanied by ashtrays. Kennji pointed out that blue was no accident; it was a color used for the logo of the GEO Group—the massive, for-profit correctional corporation that ran these facilities on behalf of their biggest client—ICE. The "O" in GEO resembled a globe, with a simple map of the world painted within it. I couldn't imagine anything worldly about a contracted security company, other than the nations represented by the people it kept detained.

"At first glance," said Kennji, "you'd think GEO ran a tight ship, but just last year it was found to be in noncompliance for being overcrowded and understaffed. Rather than build another building, they just increased security. You'll see, that's about par for the course around here." I asked Kennji if fellows repped clients from both centers. "Not since a judge last year ordered that mothers and their children be released from Karnes and the detention center at Dilley, which is a couple of hours west of here. The government still hasn't complied with that order, and because it is easier for family cases to receive funding and support, that's who we are focusing on right now. One battle at a time, right?" I wondered if this information had been handed off to Kennji, and if I would be doing the same thing in a week with the next fellow to arrive.

Once through the double set of heavy glass doors, Kennji and I entered the waiting area. The air conditioning was on high, which made me think of the *hieleras*—the short-term holding cells used by CBP along the border infamous for their freezing temperatures—that some of my clients had been detained in. The security guards, I noticed, wore jackets, and I wished I had brought one myself. To our right, there were a dozen metal lockers for storing cell phones and other belongings we weren't allowed to take into the facility with us. A metal detector and x-ray machine blocked the path down the only hallway of the facility visible to us. To the left of the metal detector, which faced the front door, there were three rows of plastic seats with minimal padding and a thick glass window with a two-way intercom. On a wall opposite them were two flat-screen TVs which played a bilingual GEO message on repeat, sharing the company's "values" with the family members or volunteers waiting to speak with the people detained here.

Kennji was already familiar with the guards and needed only to flash his ID to get in. Instead, their eyes all fell on me. "This is the new fellow," Kennji said to them, as he fished from his bag a slip of paper on which was handwritten an A-number. This he handed to a guard who looked expectantly at me for the same. I took out a list I had inherited from the previous fellow, including a few cases that she had yet to close. I read the name of the first woman on the list and the guard cut me off.

"Name doesn't help. I need the A-number. Write it down."

I jotted it down on a pad of paper. "Do I need to give you all of them?"

"No, when you are finished, you go to the guard in charge of retrieval." She nodded at Kennji. "He'll show you."

She took our slips and disappeared into the small office. Kennji put his bag into the x-ray security machine followed by a bowl with the contents of his pockets before passing through the metal detector. I repeated the procedure, its cold familiarity not lost on me. Beyond it, however, I had no idea where to go. There were no signs or directions on where I should go. The façade of being family-friendly had dissipated into the sterility of a prison. Kennji seemed acclimated to the environment, and I wondered if I would be able to do the same. At one of the few uniform doors lining the sparse hallway, Kennji stopped. "This is the pro bono room," he said. Inside was a small, windowless office furnished with a single rectangular desk surrounded by a few chairs. Other than a basic printer and a more sophisticated multitask printer—which also copied, scanned, and faxed—the room was empty. "We call it the pro bono room because volunteer lawyers can use it freely. It comes in handy for emergencies."

At the end of the hallway was a guarded door that required us to press a button. Kennji looked up at the opaque half orb of a security camera and waved. With a loud electric buzz, the door opened with a tug and we entered a small lounge area with vending machines and a refrigerator. "This is the kitchen—kind of," he said. "You can keep your lunch in the fridge, though I advise against eating here. Just grab your lunch and go eat outside. You'll have to go through security again, but it's worth it to breathe a bit before you dive back under."

The meeting room was nearby and again required being buzzed through. It was chamber-like and overseen by yet another guard. Smaller rooms branched off of it so attorneys could speak semiprivately to their clients. These pod rooms were equipped with soundproofed windows and glass doors, so while nothing could be heard—supposedly—everything was visible. Behind the guard was the waiting room where the immigrant inmates must stand by to have their identification and summons cleared. All the immigrants were assigned their own photo IDs, complete with alien registration number and room number. Even babies, which also made up a portion of the Center's population, were assigned these, not on cards, but on wristbands similar to the ones they likely received at hospitals after being born not long ago.

The guard called in the first inmate by A-number, a young woman whose case was assigned to Kennji. He introduced himself in Spanish, and they entered a room behind me. I opened the transfer memo and tried not to let this air-conditioned nightmare get to me. I made one last study of the case file and those it concerned—a mother and daughter—and let the guard know I was ready to see them. She called out their A-numbers with a dehumanizing tone, and I wondered if, or when, these numbers might be tattooed onto the skin of the undocumented immigrants. Then they appeared—a mother and her daughter hand in hand. They presented their cards to the security guard, and she checked them in. I introduced myself as a volunteer attorney, and was careful to add a *mucho gusto* when I shook the mother's hand. She returned the greeting by simply saying her name. Her daughter looked up at me with slight intimidation; no child trusts an adult at face value, and they shouldn't, but this felt especially true for the young girl who had been held in prison-like conditions with buzzers, numbers, and guards. At the urging of her mother, the three of us walked into one of the open rooms and, shutting the glass door behind us, took our seats at a cold metallic table. For a brief, claustrophobic moment, the only sound in the room was a dense silence. Finally, I flipped to a blank page in my legal pad and began where I always began, with an intake.

Monday, First Week

The immigration law I practiced in New York turned out to be very different from the work I came to learn at the detention center. Rather than immigrants who had been living undocumented in the United States or who were recently released from detention to petition for their right to stay, the inmates at Karnes City Residential Center were people who had been picked up by ICE at the border, often turning themselves in, preferring *La Migra* to an anonymous death in the desert. Women traveling with their children were sent to special and separate detention centers, like the one in Karnes City. Once there, if they stated a fear of returning to their country, they would receive either a Credible Fear Interview (CFI) or Reasonable Fear Interview (RFI)—the former being for first-time detainees without permission to enter the United States and carrying a lower standard for approval, the latter for those who have previously been deported—to be conducted by an asylum officer. The asylum officer is supposed to write everything down on special forms and read it back to the immigrant, who is then given copies of these documents. Sometimes there are translators, other times the asylum officer speaks minimal Spanish. If either the CFI or RFI come back as negative, meaning that the asylum officer does not believe that the immigrant has a reasonable or credible fear of returning to her country of origin, the immigrant can ask for an immigration judge to review the decision of the asylum officer. If the immigration judge denies the case—thus affirming the negative decision of the asylum officer—the immigrant has one last avenue, called the Request for Reconsideration (RFR), a discretionary Hail Mary, which asks the asylum office to reconsider her original, and now potentially final, decision in the case.

Preparing for the initial CFI or RFI is something that many non-lawyer volunteers assist with. For lawyers, our main job is when the immigrant asks an immigration judge to review the negative decision of the asylum office. In that case, the immigration judge reviews the record to see if there is a significant possibility that, were the negative CFI or RFI to be vacated, the immigrant could establish eligibility for asylum. In that instance, when the immigrant asks for a review of a negative CFI or RFI, the attorneys representing the immigrant mother and child have at most seven days. The regulations state that the immigration judge must conclude the review, when practicable, within twenty-four hours, but no later than seven days.

The average time from when we would first meet with a detainee to when we would appear with them before an immigration judge was three days. That may seem like a good amount of time on its face, but Maria Rogelia, the woman I had met on my first day at Karnes, was due for a hearing on Thursday, after receiving her negative CFI results the day before I arrived. Maria Rogelia was from Guerrero, a state in southwest Mexico, once known for its resort town of Acapulco, an Elvis Presley favorite. That's still there, but the region surrounding it had become a burgeoning agricultural hub for opium poppies. She recounted being raped by a gang member and then being abused by her husband. It took me the entire day to review her paperwork and conduct an intake. One day gone. I then only had two more days before the hearing. If that wasn't enough, the deadline to put together and file a brief—a ten-to-fifteen-page document with case law, facts of the current case, as well as my argument, plus another fifteen-plus pages of exhibits—was twenty-four hours before the hearing. Back in San Antonio that evening, Kennji and I shared a frozen pizza dinner before getting back to work. He was leaving that Saturday and still had three open cases. "Don't burn yourself out," he warned. "Because you're going to need energy for the other cases you'll receive. And trust me, you'll be given plenty."

Thursday, First Week

Kennji was right. In the last two days, hours had turned into minutes. I had worked seven straight hours the day before, typing, editing, and reading through my brief—seeing the client I had been assigned on my first day, who I would represent on Monday, and meeting with a new client who was challenging the negative verdict of an RFI, which had been received that morning and set for a hearing next week, which thankfully allowed me to focus this week on Maria Rogelia's case—before rereading my work, finding it sloppy, examining past briefs for help, and researching country conditions and news articles that related to my first case to include as possible exhibits—yet on the day it was due, I was unsatisfied by the brief I had assembled. If I had a week, I could have done more and better; or maybe not, maybe there was nothing else to do. One saving grace was the lawyers at RAICES who had done literally thousands of briefs and who assisted volunteer lawyers in developing them. But while they were a godsend in terms of research and general advice, the burden was still on my shoulders to deliver a plausible case. And I would be the one defending it in front of the judge.

Maria Rogelia had horrible things happen to her, but under current immigration law they did not make for a strong asylum case. It was the familiar refrain: that despite having been raped and robbed at gunpoint, her traumas weren't legally sufficient to fear returning to her country, or so the presiding Judge Cain informed us during her hearing. It is a humbling experience to hear a man, born and raised in Texas as he told me before the hearing started, tell a poor and terrified rural Mexican woman that he did not find her case credible because the asylum officer, another compassion-starved man, filed a report that told a slightly different story. At one point he even scolded her—*Get your facts straight, lady, were you raped three or four times?*—leaving her to tremble as the translator had to render this reprimand without filter. Maria Rogelia was forced to tell her traumatic story twice, to two different men who offered her no sympathy or reprieve. I couldn't imagine anything more humiliating, but given the fact that Judge Cain had one of the lowest vacate rates in the country, I shouldn't have been surprised. There seemed to be some arguments to be made in this case, and I made them: that Maria Rogelia wasn't safe in her country, nor was her daughter who, though a child, was at risk as well. But Judge Cain didn't budge. There was a discrepancy in the case that, if presented to a less rigid and heartless judge, could have made the case successful. In her report, the asylum officer noted that Maria Rogelia had stated that she had been raped by gang members. In her contestation, Maria Rogelia told me that her husband had beat her senseless for being raped, accusing her of prostitution. While domestic violence and the inability to leave an abusive relationship can be grounds for asylum—or it used to be at least—fear of gangs is considered too widespread unless you can prove the persecution is connected through a "nexus," meaning that it must have been "on account of" one of five valid grounds for asylum, and not just random or general fear. "I told the asylum officer about my husband," Maria Rogelia had told me through tears, "but she did not write this down."

And that was the trouble with asylum officer interviews. An immigrant challenging one is like an African American challenging the word of a cop. Ostensibly, these asylum officers are rigorously trained and many have backgrounds in immigration or human rights. They are well read in world affairs and study current events to know what is happening in the home countries of the people they interview. However, the interviews also occur in a setting with little to no immediate oversight. There are too many interviews conducted, supposedly, to garner additional protections that would only stretch the government resources thinner. Being able to ask the immigration judge for a review is a helpful procedure for checks on the asylum officers, but by then it is often too late. The record of the interview, unless there is something highly irregular in it, is not thoroughly questioned. If it is questioned, as I did in Maria Rogelia's case, the immigration judge will usually side with the asylum officers, giving them the benefit of the doubt that they are not misstating or misrepresenting what was said during the interview. But what if they are? For many immigration judges, an immigrant's credibility—especially those seeking asylum—is for some reason paramount to their traumas. And in cases with people at detention centers, their traumas may be so fresh that, as many psychologists have pointed out, the victim may have already repressed it, and a repressed memory cannot be recalled with reliability. For whatever reason, the judge deemed Maria Rogelia's account to lack credibility and upheld the asylum officer's assessment.

And for what? If the judge felt that Maria Rogelia had even the slightest hint of a case, she could have been sent to an immigration court in the district where she intended to relocate and had a full asylum hearing. Vacating a negative CFI granted no benefit other than release from detention and the ability to pursue her case. In Maria Rogelia's situation, the place she intended to relocate was Pittsburgh, where she had a cousin who had been more successful in finding relief some years before. Releasing her to pursue her case in Pittsburgh would not have meant a guaranteed win for her case. More importantly, her lawyer would have had more than a week to prepare briefing, greatly improving her chances of succeeding in her pursuit of asylum, of being granted withholding of removal, or of being protected under the UN–sanctioned Convention Against Torture. But the door for this possibility had been almost entirely shut for Maria Rogelia.

After the hearing, I left the court and went back to the apartment to shower off the ugliness of the result. I was then back off to Karnes. It was buzzing with volunteer activity, and when I asked one of the volunteers, a young, energetic Yale undergrad who had taken time off from classes to come and work here, what was going on, he spoke with panic. "We got four negative CFIs yesterday, it's ridiculous. We just aren't given time to prepare for each review." I picked up three of the cases, and was shocked that one hearing was scheduled for tomorrow, and the other two for Monday. "No, this isn't enough time to prepare," I said, "not at all." It was utter bullshit, but before I could even mutter that out of my breath, I had taken the cases with me back to the car. It wasn't even lunchtime and I desperately needed a stiff drink. If I were to do this full time, I thought, I'd probably end up an alcoholic. Instead I went home, ordered delivery, and started the frantic process I just finished six hours ago all over again for another detainee.

Friday, First Week

Less than twenty-four hours after Maria Rogelia's hearing, she was put on a bus with her young daughter and sent back across the border to Mexico, left at some bus stop in Laredo's Mexican counterpart, Nuevo Laredo. No matter that they knew no one in Northern Mexico, nor had any money to get back home, nearly two thousand miles away. The United States had done its job by sending Mexican nationals back to their country, and GEO would quickly find replacements to fill their beds. But because I was left ignorant of this fact, I had come to Karnes that day after Maria Rogelia's hearing ready to speak with her about how best to handle what would come next. It wasn't until I directly requested that she be brought to the meeting room (by her A-number, of course) that I was finally notified of her deportation.

"She's been shipped," said the guard looking through her roster.

"What? When?"

"Early this morning."

"Why didn't anyone notify me?"

The guard gave me an incredulous look, as if I had insulted her. "That's not our job."

"Shipped" is the actual term the government uses, as if people were packages, and ICE were mere employees of FedEx, just doing their job. As I sat there stewing, a news article I read not too long ago about an anti-immigrant protest came to mind. The photo on the first page depicted a husband and wife holding up a sign that read *Return to Sender.* Apparently, this was a widespread sentiment.

I needed a few minutes to calm myself and let the case go. Maria Rogelia was by then already across the border, when yesterday she was staring into a webcam and watching across broadband internet her life being decided by a San Antonio judge. While the lawyers appeared in the San Antonio court-room, all the women they represented made their appearances remotely from Karnes, which created a strange divide between lawyer and client. I wondered if I had rushed to Karnes and filed a stay of removal immediately after the immigration judge decided Maria Rogelia's case yesterday at 11:30 a.m. and then filed a request for reconsideration whether she and her daughter would still be here. But there were factors that were beyond my power to control. I knew that her case was weak legally, and that I had stretched my briefing as far as it would go. Maria Rogelia had unfortunately drawn the short straw in being assigned one of the more vicious immigration judges in the country. I also had to concede that Maria Rogelia was up against an increas-ingly hostile system. Immigration judges reviewing CFIs and RFIs have become wary of overburdening an already burdened immigration court system. It could also be that the immigration judge wanted to avoid a *permiso* problem, which can arise when immigrants released from detention are given their documents and explained little of the process that follows. Even though their next appearance date is on that same document, a number of immigrants were rumored to have interpreted the document as *permission* to stay in the country, period. They then suppos-edly relay this information to friends and family back home, encouraging them to come. The correlation between a misinter-preted court notice and an influx of people trying to cross the border has yet to be proved, but nonetheless, Jeh Johnson, the secretary of Homeland Security under President Obama, had to publicly address and dismiss these rumors. Were it not for the hard work of volunteers at immigration rights nonprofits like RAICES, who among many things work with recently released mothers and children to understand this process, immigration to the United States would be more fantasy than possibility. But all Maria Rogelia had received was a ride to the border. As much as I did not want to accept it, I had to move on and try to win the cases of whomever I could in the week I had left.

Saturday, Week Two

Kennji departed early in the morning. We had a beer each at a bar the evening before he left, but he also had to get things in order for the next fellow, so we returned to our rooms early. I stayed up as long as I could working on briefs for the following week. Kennji was right, though, I was burning myself out. After six straight days bustling between Karnes City Detention Center and immigration court in San Antonio, I had reached our one day off. Though I needed to be here when the next fellow arrived, that wouldn't be until the midafternoon. With half the day to myself, I decided against Kennji's suggestion to head to Austin and instead planned a drive to see the actual border with my own eyes. Despite a short night of sleep, I rose early and was at a brunch spot by 8:00 a.m., eating a breakfast sandwich and washing it down with a virgin Bloody Mary. I'd have to do without the kick of alcohol for now. Instead I grabbed a cup of coffee to go, got into my car heating under the morning sun, put "Laredo" into Google Maps, and entered onto the nearby I-35 freeway for a nearly three-hour journey through southwestern Texas to the end of America.

In the weeks before coming to Texas, I had binge-read border novels by writers like Cormac McCarthy and Larry McMurtry, which had given me a visual idea of the region. To see its rich detail as I drove toward Laredo, though, was at times unexpected and mesmerizing. In some aspects, southwestern Texas was a continuation of the cattle country that surrounded Karnes, yet the landscape itself was distinct from it. For much of the drive, the only upright things in sight were prickly pear cacti and old fence posts with rusted barbed wire that rolled along the khaki and orange dirt occasionally interrupted by wisps of green earth. They reminded me most of the setting of McMurtry's famous border novel *Lonesome Dove*.

In place of the cowboys who roamed on horseback over the romantic, unsettled lands of the West were small towns like Falls City, which I'd miss if I blinked. Yet I'd learned by then that a small town didn't necessarily mean big things couldn't hide there. An hour outside of San Antonio, I passed the exit for Dilley, a small Texas town once locally famous for its enormous watermelons. Since 2014, however, its name had become notorious in immigration rights circles for housing the largest family immigrant detention center in the United States. Dilley is by all standards a prison that houses up to 2,400 immigrants, many of whom are mothers and their children. The "private rooms" where they are housed are cells that cram in multiple families. And like the Karnes Residential Center, it was given a cheery name fit for a retirement community: the South Texas Family Residential Center. The branding of immigrant detention was no different than any other polemic issue in American politics, but no matter what you called a turd, you still couldn't polish it.

Though Dilley and Karnes were pretty similar their differences were notable, the main one being that the latter was a licensed childcare facility while the former was not. Nor is Dilley a GEO-run facility, rather it is owned and operated by Corrections Corporation of America (CCA; renamed Core-Civic in 2016), another billion-dollar company thriving off the privatization of prisons and their government contracts. The icing on that cake was that Dilley was not the only immigration detention facility in America to illegally house children. Pro-immigration and children's rights advocates had been vocal for years in demanding these family detention centers be shut down, and one of the main arguments they used was through the *Flores* settlement, which barred undocumented youth from being held for more than twenty days in secure detention facilities without trying to place them with a legal guardian and that such facilities must meet child welfare standards, meaning they must be licensed. The Obama Administration had decided not to separate families during this time period and was thus keeping them detained together for indefinite periods of time, well beyond the limits in the *Flores* settlement, and they were being detained in unlicensed and secure facilities. Though children being detained with their mothers were not technically unaccompanied, in July of 2015, lawyers for the *Flores* settlement argued that they should be protected in the same manner—and a federal judge agreed, finding that the *Flores* settlement applied equally to unaccompanied minors as well as children detained with their parents, meaning that those children in Karnes and Dilley still had rights to be housed in the "least restrictive setting" (a description that no person would ascribe to Karnes or other family detention centers). The fact that a judge could make this finding and issue an order, however, is never a guarantee that the government would fully comply with it.

An hour later, the ranches disappeared and in their place were signs of more recent molding by human hands. Large warehouses and industrial parks were the first to appear, until finally the landscape burst forth with a miracle mile of American franchises and excess—Walmart, Olive Garden, Target, Best Buy, Fuddruckers, Ford dealerships, Best Western, Western Sizzlin'— a long, deep-fried American goodbye that escorted you right into downtown Laredo, where the franchises abruptly ceased and Mexico began. I wondered how often Mexicans had easily come in the other direction, whether they had felt that the United States had placed before them a welcome mat of corporations that made millions selling people things they didn't need, and whether they too would get to partake in the hedonism.

I-35 ended near the Juarez-Lincoln International Bridge, which crosses the border at the Rio Grande. I parked near the Greyhound bus station and made my way down to the river. The entire downtown area seemed to be under construction, for sale, or occupied by discount vendors. Bulk deals were everywhere for knock-off brand apparel, sports gear, electronics, and personal-care products; signs for *mayoreo* (wholesale) and *menudeo* (retail) filled dozens of shop windows. I wandered in the direction of the Rio Grande, passing a direction sign for the Laredo Border Heritage Museum. I tried to imagine what heritage a border could have, but before I could dwell on it, I came to the river, which was much bigger, browner, and faster than I had expected. Yet it wasn't wide enough to make Mexico seem all that far—about half the distance than Brooklyn was from Manhattan. But it felt different—I could see a Gateway to the Americas Duty-Free shop adjacent to a security crossing, a line of cars waiting to be inspected and checked, and, in a riverside park, a basketball court so close to the river that people on its opposite banks could enjoy a game.

I spotted a man who resembled a young Nicolas Cage, mustache and all, in a border patrol uniform slowly pacing the park. I wasn't sure why he was there, perhaps to guard it from anyone who might try to swim across the Rio Grande, or maybe just to take a break from his work. Still, I wandered over to him and instinctively asked in Spanish for taco joint recommendations.

Ever since I stepped out of my car, all I had read and heard had been in Spanish, and not surprisingly, he gave a fluent reply, boasting of the tacos at a stand only a couple blocks away. The irony of having addressed in Spanish a white American tasked with keeping out brown-skinned Mexicans about where to find the best tacos did not immediately strike me, but when it did, it only furthered my belief that borders were illusory, particularly when it came to food.

The taco stand, which took five minutes to reach and five minutes more to find, was a storefront, with two windows, one of which was partially blocked by a Coca-Cola vending machine. Only the lime-green menu, painted on the storefront had given it away. Feeling a little overwhelmed by the selection—over a dozen taco options, a few *platillos,* and a selection of *licuados*— I asked the man taking orders what's good and he recommended something not on the painted menu: a spicy mess of meat, chili, potatoes, and refried beans. I ordered four along with a bottled water, then took my lunch to a nearby plaza, with the large San Agustin cathedral in front of me and the Spanish colonial splendor of La Posada Hotel behind me.

After I ate, I decided to set out for the Border Heritage Museum, which, like the taco stand, took only a few minutes to reach. The museum was small, a single room that occupied an old merchant's home. The exhibits displayed copies of documents and photographs regarding the history of the U.S.–Mexican border, as well as a map that shows the extent of Mexico before it ceded half of its land to the United States, a time when the Mexican-American border was not south but west, reaching as far north as Oregon and as deep as Wyoming. While I didn't have time to take it all in, the historic relationship between Laredo and Nuevo Laredo caused me to linger. When the Mexican-American War "officially" ended on Groundhog Day of 1848 with the signing of the Treaty of Guadalupe-Hidalgo—or, as it is officially and absurdly titled, the Treaty of Peace, Friendship, Limits and Settlement between the United States of America and the Mexican Republic—many border towns were given the option to remain or leave the United States. At the time of the treaty and due to its proximity to the Rio Grande, however, Laredo had been occupied by a U.S. military garrison, making the town American by *defacto*. A petition by its residents to return Laredo to Mexico was met with deaf ears. This prompted a sizeable amount of the town's populace, who wished to remain Mexican, to cross the river and found Nuevo Laredo in May of that same year.

My final plan of the day was to cross the border on foot and walk around Nuevo Laredo, comparing the new with the old, two cities unilaterally connected despite the natural boundary of a water line. Wallet and passport in hand, I began the walk toward the checkpoint on the nearby bridge. I was about halfway through, when I noticed the charcoal-colored clouds that seemed to be churning above me. Drops of rain started pelting the corrugated steel covering the walkway, until they pounded it with violence. I heard thunder, saw a flash of light, and became mindful of lightning striking the metal. I looked toward Nuevo Laredo growing hazy in the torrential downpour. I glanced back at Laredo and saw the same image. Cars on both sides flapped their windshield wipers. Guards ducked for cover. Below me, the Rio Grande bulged with water, incorporating the ceaseless raindrops into its flow. Because mother nature did not discriminate based on political boundary, no side seemed any more likely to break with sunlight than the other. And yet that was what the border represented to so many people—one side was seen to offer a sunnier life than the other, even if it rained on both.

Monday, Week Two

Sam, the new fellow, was an attorney with a varied caseload and practice areas. His arrival meant that I was now the veteran fellow, and that it was my duty to guide Sam in the way that Kennji had guided me. At first I felt uncomfortable with the position, and slightly intimidated by my predecessor's ability to pass on knowledge with ease. I took Sam out to the BBQ joint to break bread, or ribs, rather, just as Kennji had done with me. Before long we had settled into conversation, and I found it comforting to hear that Sam's questions were very much in the same vein as my own a week before. But like Kennji had once cautioned me, I warned him about the work that lay ahead, and tried to communicate that while he should remain hopeful, he ought to be mentally prepared to be gutted.

Within two hours after arriving at Karnes, Sam picked up two cases with hearings only a couple days later. My caseload had been expanded to include another five, each one with troubling peculiarities. Ursula, a Salvadoran mother, and her five-year-old son were given an asylum interview. As was so often the circumstance, the woman had been raped right before the boy's eyes by a gang member who threatened to kill the child if he said a word to anyone. The mother, for one reason or another, was more comfortable telling the story through the boy's eyes and did not mention immediately that the gang member had also threatened her. The mother had initially asked that the boy not be in the room so as not to hear and relive these details, but she relayed them to the asylum officer who called the boy in and asked him several questions. Whatever the reason, his responses made the asylum officer believe that only the boy was eligible for asylum. Or else it was a mistake, a life-altering checking of the wrong box.

When I spoke with her, she remained reluctant to allow her young son, only a few years older than my own two-year-old daughter, to hear the story she so agonizingly retold. I didn't have the heart to tell her that his innocence had already been tainted. I gave him paper and crayons that the RAICES volunteer had brought to the waiting room, and off he went to the meeting room area to draw on the metallic table at its center. Later I found out that these same crayons had been banned at Karnes due to "destruction of property." They had been using them to color over the white, sterilized walls in the visitor's area with streaks of forest green or deep ocean blue. It seemed unnecessarily cruel for a billion-dollar company like GEO to wish to maintain pristine sterility at the expense of a child's pleasure.

The child slept with his mother and other mothers and their children in a cell with thin bunk beds, and like all the children in the cell and that I met, he coughed from deep in his chest and had eternal strings of snot hanging from his nose. The children were thin, somehow having lost weight since their journey here. At Dilley, two years later in 2018, a little girl became very ill and apparently did not receive proper treatment she needed while detained. After being released with her mother, she was soon thereafter hospitalized, and six weeks after they had been released from Dilley the little girl died.

Another mother, Raquel, assured me that a cousin in Houston had hired a private attorney for her, and that it would be him, not me, who would represent her at the hearing on Wednesday. I was dubious, as I always was, whenever a client hired a private attorney. In Raquel's case, the guy had not even come to speak with her despite having already taken a $500 cash payment for a retainer. Nor did she know his name or contact information. Still, she seemed confident that the hearing on Wednesday would result in a favorable verdict. I didn't share this sentiment, yet I saw no point in bursting her bubble. Instead, I told her that I would be in court on Wednesday for another case if she needed me, and that just in case her attorney was a no-show, I would make sure to ask the judge if I could step in or to grant a continuance, at least for one more day so I could prepare something for her case.

I was discovering too the disregard for the humanity of those detained at Karnes. Rather than say "women and children" or "inmates" or "detainees" the guards tasked with processing, transporting, and watching over them referred to them as "bodies." I overheard on several occasions someone shouting "I need to take a body count." It was as if the guards had numbed themselves to such a degree that they could only see these women and children as dead people walking. I guess, in a sense, they were dead women and children walking, especially those who had lost their cases and were due to be deported. Or maybe a commission for each "body" counted was paid to the guards, as it certainly was by DHS to GEO and CCA. When I first read *Between the World and Me*, Ta-Nehisi Coates's lyrical treatise on the transient nature and mistreatment of black bodies, this term hinted at larger historical and present-day parallels with the immigrant community. This is the "visceral experience" of racism that Coates speaks of, now infusing immigrant lives.

That the immigration system is flawed and prejudiced is an unfortunate truth of bureaucracy, but the depth of its faults was unfathomable. Erica was one of the detention center's longest residents. She had been assigned the same immigration judge assigned to Maria Rogelia, the mother from Guerrero, who had also affirmed the asylum officer's negative assessment. Unlike me, who made the crucial misstep of waiting a day to file a Request for Reconsideration, her pro bono attorney had done so immediately. She had been awaiting the results of that request for nearly six months. Not until I was assigned her case did she have any movement on it, and that was only because her sister, who lived on Long Island, figured out where she was and called the RAICES office only a week prior. Because there is no list of detainees provided to attorneys, RAICES relies on family members reaching out to them and other means of learning who is detained and wants to speak with an attorney. But not long after I began compiling a briefing, her hearing was halted. Erica and her daughter were being transferred from Karnes to the Berks Detention Center in Pennsylvania, another notorious family detention center. I was able to see Erica before she left, and she told me that no matter how bad it was to be detained here in the States, it was still better than returning to El Salvador. I wondered if another few months at Berks would change her mind.

The pro bono room became a sanctuary of sorts to retreat to after the coldness and claustrophobia of the meeting rooms. I could be alone there, take a deep breath, collect my thoughts, and fart, one of life's small comforts. I'd even let the door open and hoped the smell wafted toward the guards nearby, a minor punishment for their complicity in detaining families. I wondered if the whole facility had been designed to intentionally intimidate the detainees—large steel bolts clacked to open and shut the heavy-set metal doors; the rooms were windowless and buzzed with fluorescent lighting; and one could always feel the scrutiny of the guards through the inter-room glass partitions. I wondered at times about the humanity of these guards, whether at the end of the day, they got to go home to their own families. Only one seemed remotely friendly, a chatty fourth-generation Texan whose ancestors, according to her, were among those who stayed behind in Laredo during the mass exodus that formed Nuevo Laredo. Small talk aside, a guard was still a guard, and sometimes just their presence felt oppressive.

I spoke with another attorney who had arrived at the detention center earlier that week. Melanie was an attorney in her midthirties who, through the funding and hospitality of online donors, traveled the country from detention center to detention center, providing legal services to undocumented immigrants and documenting the entire length and breadth of the immigrant experience. At the time, she was only two months into her journey, with all of her belongings, including a tent that she often used, stuffed into a two-seater Smart car, but support for her project was quickly growing. While working pro bono at Karnes, the pro-immigrant sisters of a convent had offered her room and board as well as wisdom and prayer. She described the convent's modest accommodations and strict alcohol-free environment when I suggested grabbing a beer after work. Instead, she left me inspired to do something similar, and I even suggested to Alejandra that we could strap Chloe into a car seat and spend the next year vagabonding as volunteers at detention centers like Karnes. She entertained the idea for a few minutes, excited about a new adventure. Then she told me how her actual job search had been going.

Tuesday, Week Two

If people like Melanie kept my optimism up, asylum officers like Craig brought it right back down. Craig was the kind of person who took pleasure in giving negative results in the interviews he conducted. The Credible Fear Interview was supposed to assess whether immigrants had something to fear were they to be sent back to their country, but more often, the women I spoke with also credibly feared him, including a woman named Brenda who described her harrowing encounter with Craig:

"I walked into his office and he told me to 'sit down.' He

didn't say his name or ask what my name was or my son's. Then he said: 'I'm going to ask you some stupid questions, and you already know the answers.' I didn't understand. Why would I already know the answers? When he started asking the questions, my son and I were confused because we didn't know who should answer. When I asked him, he yelled my name. Then I tried to answer a question and he yelled 'That wasn't for you!' He could tell we were scared and he said 'No one here will bite,' and then laughed. I asked him to say a question again, and he asked my son and I if we were asleep and then he laid his head down on his desk and pretended to be asleep and then he started laughing again. Then he stopped letting us talk and said 'I know what you're going to say,' whenever I tried to answer a question about the reasons I left El Salvador. Then he said that he was done with us, that we would have to see him again and answer his questions correctly before he could finish the interview."

Craig sounded to me like a sadist, the kind of person who would laugh at a lynching. For Brenda, it was utterly humiliating. But rather than cower at his misanthropy, she was so galvanized by her fury that after the interview, she approached one of the officials from the detention center and relayed the same story she was telling me. This set off a strange chain of events. Brenda was never called back for another interview with Craig, who had clearly crossed a line. And yet, the process was never corrected. Craig won out: his initial interview result, which stated that he had not found Brenda's fear of returning to El Salvador credible, went through. She and her son did not get another interview. I was able, however, to represent her, and I began planning on ways to document and challenge this incident and the interview results.

I was concerned that other interviews with Craig were likely done without proper conduct. That evening, I wrote to Barbara

Hines, a border legend who is supposedly retired from immigration law but keeps at it, about the day's decision and the worrying circumstances I had seen. I included information on two other Craig-related cases I was then working on, and expressed my anxiety that I wouldn't have time to protect others from a malicious interviewer. In the morning, I received a reply from Barbara, who expressed deep concern and offered to look into the matter. I was to expect to hear back from her by the end of that day.

Wednesday, Week Two

The San Antonio immigration court did in fact have its own version of Judge Vargas. Judge Torres had a reputation for vacating negative CFIs on even the weakest of cases, reasoning that she would rather the mothers be able to present a full case rather than a rushed one, especially those heard without an attorney to represent them. I wanted to believe that she shared my distrust of asylum officers and the initial asylum process, but whatever inspired her decisions, any volunteer or pro bono attorney working with detained mothers and children delighted in seeing her name beside that of their client. When I saw that Karen, the youngest mother I was to represent, had been assigned Judge Torres, I was relieved the immigration judge roulette had worked in our favor this time.

As much as I appreciated the benevolence of judges like Judge Torres, I would've rather the system not be left to the personal bias of whoever is sitting on the bench. But that's more or less how the system has worked—an immigrant is either in the right place before the right judge or the wrong place before the wrong judge, with a combination of the two making up an increasingly minority middle. To put it another way, an immigrant seeking asylum would have a much better chance in New York immigration court than one in say, Atlanta, with exactly the same case facts. According to activist organization Advocacy For Human Rights in the Americas, "judges in New York grant asylum in more than 75 percent of the cases, in Atlanta almost 90 percent of asylum requests are denied."

An increasingly violent world means an exploding number of people hoping to receive refuge from it. El Salvador and Honduras consistently rank in the top five most violent countries in the world, and with that violence, especially from gangs like MS-13 and Barrio 18 that have mandatory lifetime memberships and wield outsized power akin to that of a federal government, comes fear of retribution for those returned to their countries. If a judge in New York City could find that, under current asylum law and based on the brief filed by the attorney, a Salvadoran qualified for asylum, it was completely unfair and undoubtedly prejudicial that a judge in Atlanta could not find the same and also grant asylum.

But that day, speaking before Judge Torres, I could breathe a sigh of relief. Not only had she vacated the negative CFI as I had hoped, but she had done so despite berating me for interrupting the proceedings to correct the court translator. Never did translation seem so important to be correct, yet our interlocutor messed up a crucial point about the type of abuse she had faced at the hands of her husband. Though the judge questioned this detail and admonished the young mother for perceived credibility issues not included in the asylum officer's report, her chastisement did not prevent her from declaring a verdict in my client's favor. When I asked my client where she planned to go now that she would be released, her reply depressed me. "I'm going to live with my brother, who lives in Atlanta," she said. Karen will be put on a bus thinking that hell (Honduras) and its gates (Karnes) will forever be behind her. But worse, feasibly much worse, than the hell she has lived through, is glimpsing the gates of heaven and then being torn away forever: losing her asylum case in the toughest jurisdiction in the country once she has settled in with her brother in Georgia and put the violence she suffered in Honduras behind her.

Friday, Week Two

It was my last day at Karnes and I needed a victory. Since Karen's CFI had been vacated, I had lost the following two cases, and I had two more today, the last two I would have before my time in Texas would come to an end. I slept badly the previous night—Craig, the menacing asylum officer, had been the asylum officer who had given both the two clients who had cases today negative reviews and was somehow still allowed to do his job. Barbara Hines, however, as she was famous for doing, came through. She had not only sent a scathing letter to the USCIS director of Refugee, Asylum and International Operations but had also completed a declaration and gathered more facts on all the cases that had had an interview before Craig. On top of that, she knew the judge I would be appearing before that day. "I think she'll vacate when she sees this information."

She was right. I won both the cases, but in the second case, a hearing for Juanita, a Guatemalan mother of three, the triumph was emotional. When the judge stated her decision, Juanita started sobbing and I could see through the video that she was gripping her chair. Through her tears, she thanked me, thanked the judge, thanked the United States and God. Juanita's destination was, of all places, a distant cousin's home in New York City. While I spoke with her over video, I told her my phone number to contact me when she arrived in New York City. The judge looked away and shuffled papers in the folder. I could tell she hadn't anticipated how affected she would be by her decision, made over the course of only ten minutes. I hoped that she would carry this moment with her to the thousands of cases awaiting her in the future.

Sam and I celebrated with a couple of beers each. It was my last day as the veteran fellow. In the back of my mind, however, I could feel the encroachment of guilt. I had lost more cases than I had won, and flashes of Maria Rogelia's sudden deportation stuck with me. I tried not to think of what had happened since their deportation, whether they were able to accept it, whether they returned to better circumstances, or whether their deportation had also been their death sentence. While Sam and I celebrated a great day, the hundreds of inmates back at Karnes were surely praying for theirs. I wanted to return home, and every single one of them did not. I had the familiar recurrence, the juxtaposition of my wife and daughter with the immigrants I work with. Alejandra and Chloe were in New York City, in a comfortable apartment, two bedrooms and one bathroom; and Elvira and her daughter, the last case I lost, were likely a month or more away from being sent back to El Salvador. They would spend that month waiting in a cramped cell with another mother and child. I think of the children I spoke with in Karnes, excited about the paper and crayons I lent them, something to play with and focus on instead of the cold walls slowly closing in on them, eventually pushing them out, back across the desert they traversed just weeks ago.

My flight from San Antonio did not take me back to the border, only farther and farther away from it. I had been in Texas only two weeks, yet it felt like a lifetime had passed and the memories branded on to me. I knew now why Cormac McCarthy set so many of his books in the borderlands—it haunted you, like the space underneath your childhood bed, a space between comfort and reality. It would take months to shake this place, if I ever did. Or if I ever should. Some things a person needs to carry through life with them, and I suspected that these days along the border would be such for me. More poignantly, it affected how I perceived the long-revered American Dream, espoused when convenient and otherwise either a myth or applied to only a select few. I left the border knowing more about immigrant lives and immigration law and less about the United States. The only truth I was sure of on my last day at the border was that the nation obsessed with God blessing it had become decidedly ungodly. Prayers are fading quickly, somewhere not far from the quixotic lips of the immigrant women who whisper them nightly in their cells, perhaps in the dust surrounding Karnes County Residential Center, a jail for immigrant mothers and children, but also a graveyard of hopes and American Dreams.

PART IV

OUR AMERICA

. . . .

Podrán cortar todas las flores, pero no podrán detener la primavera.

(They can cut all the flowers, but they can't stop spring from coming.)

—*Pablo Neruda*

One Thursday morning later that fall, I walked over to a Sunset Park–based elementary school nearby to give a Know-Your-Rights presentation to a PTA group of concerned Asian and Latino parents. While a majority of deportations from the United States are of people from Mexico and Central America, a sizable demographic of deportees are from China and the Philippines. They all have one thing in common: fear. Donald Trump had just been elected president, and the parents who had been scared of Obama's inability to enforce his pro-immigration orders were now terrified of a man outspokenly anti-immigrant. While he had yet to take office, the sentiment in the immigration communities was the same: that ICE would become more powerful and more menacing. The focus of that morning's event was to address that trepidation and provide advice on what to do. The school had a large auditorium and every seat was filled, with a natural segregation dividing the room into Latino and Asian sides. I had not eaten breakfast and was running primarily on adrenaline and caffeine. While I had grown comfortable speaking before a court, where I could direct my attention to the judge, I was more nervous speaking to a large crowd of people. Two interpreters would be relaying everything I said into their microphones—an elderly man provided Mandarin and a younger woman did the same for Spanish.

For my presentation, I focused on the continued threat of ICE, on avoiding detention, and what to do if detained. I did my best to not sound alarmist and reiterated everything I said with assurances such as "Until you are physically deported, you have options." But dread was very present in the room, and while some people jotted down notes, many more seemed to look at me with despair in their hearts. The ICE raids under Obama had shaken everyone into thinking that the next knock on their door would be from the fist of an ICE agent. One of my main points was to make sure everyone, even children, were prepared for the worst. If you are detained and a child does not know what to do, make a family plan, I stressed. It was time for their kids to know what's going on, because if a parent was detained, a child needs to know what to do. Make sure the name and number of an immigration attorney and a temporary guardian of your choice—preferably someone your kid can identify—are written down where your child knows where to find them. You may also want to leave some cash or a prepaid debit card in case your child needs money. By preparing for the worst, and by planning as a family, you will have the best chance of getting out of a bad situation, or, at the very least, not making a bad situation worse—if the tragedy of a deportation can really be deemed a bad situation.

Council member Menchaca was to be the next speaker, with two more after him, including a woman from a Brooklyn-based immigration advocacy group and another woman, a working mother of two, who had been detained and later released by ICE. Countless hands shot up after I ended my presentation, but the event's officiant notified everyone that things needed to keep moving. A children's book author was scheduled to give a reading to the students after we all spoke. I recognized the author's name from my trips to the bookstore with Chloe. Once again, the normalcy of life enjoyed by so many families, including my own, oddly contrasted to the thought of deportation that terrorized many others. I looked over at the principal who, from a previous presentation I gave that ended in a marathon Q & A session, had come prepared. She informed the parents that following the conclusion of the other speakers, an assembly for questions would be held in the children's library on the floor above the auditorium.

Thirty minutes later, I walked into the library, where people were already filing in and taking seats on brightly colored beanbags that lay underneath large portraits of Clifford the Big Red Dog and Arthur and other favorites that lined the walls and hovered above the bookshelves. Other people crammed into the small seats that surrounded the six tables in the center of the room. I was ten minutes early, yet people appeared to stare at me with impatience as I wolfed down my sandwich. The principal finally arrived and closed the doors to the library behind her. The same interpreters as before took their place, though because people had grabbed whatever seats were available, the library was much less segregated. None of the other speakers were present, so the principal gave me a brief introduction, then walked back toward the door where she stood, arms folded.

I began by explaining that the only questions I could answer were ones that might benefit everyone in the room, general questions relating to rights during an ICE raid, or debunking rumors spreading through the community, because questions concerning individual cases would require me to study their facts to them to give a proper answer. "That's for your lawyer to answer," I said, "not just any lawyer." I watched as the interpreters relayed my message, hoping that what I stressed would be translatable. And then the floor was opened to the audience.

Inevitably, individual-case questions were the first to be asked. A Chinese mother in her late twenties inquired about the specifics of her asylum claim, asking when she will have a response on her application. A Honduran father who had hired a lawyer for an upcoming case wanted to know the chances of getting a U visa. Again and again I explained that *I cannot answer specific questions about your case*, repeating the phrase like a mantra, and offering advice that related more broadly to the issues their cases broached. It's not that I didn't want to help, it's that there are no easy questions when it comes to immigration cases. Just as an intake presents a different set of circumstances for each person, so does each case. Plus, if they were already represented by an attorney, the ethics of giving legal advice were problematic.

One benefit of being asked individual questions, even if I couldn't answer them, was that everyone in the room began to understand that they were not alone in their plight, and like a group therapy session, this gave a certain strength to talk openly about their cases and their lives. A person's story, summarized as *I came to the U.S. in 2007, was deported after I was arrested in 2010, and then I came back and crossed the next month,* would be shared with the rest of the group, despite openly admitting to a federal crime, punishable with several years in prison before inevitable deportation. They did not feel shy, burdened, or uncomfortable in sharing this information because everyone was for the most part in the same situation, or empathized because they knew that could be them at any moment.

One Mexican mother's question on her case touched upon a pattern of concern I had begun noticing, and it gave me pause enough to address it. It concerned removal proceedings and immigration lawyer hoodwinking. The woman was undocumented and had resided undocumented in the United States for over ten years, and had a son who was not only a citizen but had a disability that required her to be hyper-attentive to him. She even had to find someone qualified to take care of him in order for her to come here. The woman was working under the table but needed more money and stability, so she sought out an immigration lawyer to advise her on getting her proper work authorization. In turn, he told her to fill out an application for a special visa—the Ten Year Visa, the attorney called it—that would get her a work permit and eventually, a green card.

"And soon after I applied, I got my work authorization," she said, and then with a tone of frustration, "I received a paper telling me to go to the immigration court not long after that, and the court date is in a few weeks. What happened? What do I do?"

I could guess at what had happened. The immigration lawyer who had gotten her a work authorization had likely done so by filing a false asylum application. I say false because likely the immigrant didn't truly qualify for asylum, and usually, with rare exceptions, only someone applying within the first year after arrival qualified for it. Once immigrants lose their asylum claim—which they will, since that's the point—their application is sent to immigration court and they are put in removal proceedings, where the attorney will apply for Non-Lawful Permanent Resident (LPR) Cancellation of Removal. This form of relief is a last ray of hope for longtime residents to obtain lawful status. If they can meet certain requirements, their removal proceedings will be canceled, and they may receive a green card—but they have to be put into removal proceedings first to qualify. It is also a discretionary form of relief, and if the immigration judge presiding over the removal proceedings does not feel that the immigrant has met his or her burden in fulfilling the requirements, the immigrant will be deported. Ultimate reward, ultimate risk. But because immigration lawyers aren't always transparent with how they plan to proceed with a case, the client often has no idea what is going on and won't know about the risk, like the Mexican mother. The false asylum claim and the very real risk of deportation go unmentioned.

I considered how to be honest and gentle with my answer, but what came out was raw truth: "There is no such thing as a ten-year visa."

Her face immediately contorted with confusion, but I continued. "I can't be sure what you applied for, but it seems like you have been put into removal proceedings." The words "removal proceedings" even untranslated, got everyone's attention. The mother had the stony look of someone trying to digest a shocking event.

"Being in removal proceedings does not mean certain deportation," I said, looking at her. "You can still apply for Non-LPR Cancellation of Removal, which I think may be your attorney's plan. It is a petition to be taken off of the removal docket. If a judge grants the cancellation, you become eligible for a green card, depending on your circumstances."

This seemed to slightly reinvigorate her, but now she seemed fragile, and many other people were visibly concerned. And the worst news, that the petition was discretionary, would have been cruel to relay. Yet that too was true: if a judge did not feel the immigrant had met certain criteria to be granted cancellation, the immigrant would be out of options and would be detained and scheduled for deportation. As the news sunk into the room, the woman once again spoke up.

"You know, I don't care anymore. If I get a green card, great, but if not, I'll keep my bags packed. If they deport me, I'll just go live with my mother anyway, who can look after my son while I'm at work. And anyway, Trump can kiss my ass," she triumphantly stated. Parents around her laughed as the interpreters translated this bit. I laughed as well. It's a sentiment that everyone in the room shared, but then a thought occurred to me. Why shouldn't more lawyers attempt to exploit this loophole, and every loophole for that matter? Being an immigration lawyer is like always bringing a knife to a gun fight, and now, against an administration intent on building a "big beautiful wall" to keep people out of this country and using every means necessary to rid it of immigrants, why not play dirty, if the immigrant is aware of the risks? If our usual blades are to grow dull, maybe it's the shanks and dirks that we should depend on to have a fighting chance.

But addressing individual fears is easier than navigating the collective fear that plagues many mixed-status families. While children born on U.S. soil of undocumented mothers and fathers are citizens by virtue of that birthright, this ensures nothing for their parents. It is only when citizens turn twenty-one that they have the right to apply for their parents to become permanent residents. Members of Congress have derogatorily referred to such citizens as "anchor babies," and the Trump administration has broached the idea of changing the Constitution to remove birthright citizenship. Yet most of the children of those gathered here were young enough to be back down in the auditorium, enraptured by a children's story. An undocumented parent would have to somehow exist here under an unlawful status, long before his or her child reaches government-approved adulthood, to find a legal route to relief. And even then, with at least twenty-one years of unlawful status, the parent would have to apply for special waivers to even be eligible for the child's sponsorship.

The legal issues of split-status families, however, were secondary. A team at George Washington University found elevated rates of anxiety and PTSD among parents and children in a 2018 report, due largely to looming and constant threats of deportation. Children like those attending this school say goodbye to their parents each morning and suffer until the bell rings, rushing home to see if their parents are still there. Teachers, both in the GWU study and among those I speak with at the school, notice that poor performance is more common and behavioral issues have grown exponentially in the short time since Trump's election. The Civil Rights Project at UCLA published a working paper with similar findings, noting that "psychologists have found negative effects on cognitive development and educational progress among school age children with unauthorized parents, even where the children are U.S. citizens." The effects are broad and long-term, with some analysts suggesting that these mental health issues will be borne by society at-large, with higher healthcare costs and increased stress on the criminal justice system.

And then there are some parents who are convinced it is time to move on. I heard from a couple that told me they were planning on returning to Mexico and taking their U.S.–citizen children with them. "I don't want to be here. I live in fear," the mother said. "I'd rather be back in Guatemala and at least be able to go outside and live my life," another mother said, preferring to risk facing gang violence than staying here undocumented. The other parents gave her a round of applause. People were ready to give up on the United States more than ever before, even if they had waited years to ensure their kids got an American education, were accepted into an American university, and could live out the dream that they could not. What was once the light of the world has become a dark place, one that a growing number of people think best to leave.

The douser of the flicker of freedom was, of course, Trump. The man who wanted his name on everyone's lips had ironically gotten his wish, especially within the immigrant community. Once the parents started talking about him, they could not stop, and my participation in the Q & A went from expert and adviser to commentator and therapist. I explained that there are certain things that a president can do on his own, through Executive Orders, but many things that must go through Congress. This did little to comfort anyone, yet of the many concerns I heard, it was rumors that most exacerbated fear. People had heard that Trump would rescind DACA completely, and that all immigrants, no matter their status, would be deported under his new administration. I tried to calm their worries by telling them that a rumor was not a law, and that I specialized in the latter and not the former. "You didn't come to America to fear it," I said. "And if a district court judge can overturn Obama's presidential order, then another judge can overturn a similar but opposite order by Trump." I couldn't have known then how prescient I was being, or that many of the rumors would become facts.

After the Q & A, I handed out my card and thanked the parents for attending. It was difficult to discern from their faces if I had brought them any clarity or had made them more confused. Only the principal carried a smile, and as she shook my hand, she promised to be in touch to discuss making these meetings a monthly event. I walked out the front door and into the cold, through the grass and courts until I came to a set of cobblestone stairs that gave expansive views to Sunset Park. I descended the steps and exited onto Fifth Avenue. The office was not far, but my head was full of self-analysis. I wondered if I had been too pessimistic or blunt, if it was possible to sugarcoat more things at the next training. But the truth was, even I didn't know what was in store for their rights, and I realized that any false optimism would be a disservice. *Hope* was the mantra from the previous administration. *Making America Great Again* was the slogan for the incumbent one, and it was not designed to be inclusive of everyone who lived here. And for those excluded by that promise, and for those who fought on their behalf, it was now time to plan for the worst.

=====

Like so many people who watched the election on November 8, 2016, its recollection pains me. I remember watching Wolf Blitzer on CNN stand in front of a map of the United States of America redden with tortuous patience. Like so many people who watched the election with fading hope, I didn't stay tuned in to hear the final call, and I had no interest in Hillary's concession or Trump's victory speech. This could all not be happening, I told myself as I went to bed, hoping to wake up to another reality, which of course I did. As the nation would find out, this reality brought along with it a return to a more hateful America. I knew our country had its prejudices, I had seen it growing up with an immigrant mother, but I had never seen them flaunted so publicly.

At a dinner with British friends the night after the Brexit vote, I had laughed and joked at their misery, laying into Boris Johnson and Nigel Farage. I saw the United States on its path to its first female president, and after dinner that night I even went home and whispered to my daughter in her crib that now it was true: she could be anything. I repeatedly asked our British friends at dinner "What happened?"—cruelly unaware that this would later be the title of the Hillary Clinton autopsy of her campaign. The Brits were too dejected to answer until after a few drinks, when one of them supplied the only clear answer of the night: "Wait until November. You'll see, anything can happen in this post-truth world." I shrugged off her comments; no seed of doubt was ever sown. I had repeated to every one of my clients: he won't win, he won't win and he will never win—and I believed it blindly. But they knew better than me. They know America, and more importantly, Americans, better than anyone. They toil in her fields, sweat in her kitchens, absorb her worst abuses, and return the next day to begin again. From this, they have come to know a truth that many of us ignore or refuse to believe: America, the ideal, the hope that the immigrant came for, is very different and perhaps permanently divorced from American actions. The immigrants I spoke with during the campaign saw clearly a man cultivating this chasm, calling for their demise, and they understood it would propel him to the presidency.

But like so many people, after having the rug pulled from under me and my smugness handed to me, I somehow found strength to get back up and put my voice to use. The same weekend Trump was elected to the executive office, a massive protest march was held in which thousands marched from the southwest entrance to Central Park at Columbus Circle down to Trump Tower. Alejandra, Chloe, and I went out to participate as a family, to be with the immigrant community I defended and for whom Alejandra provides psychological services. Many parents had made similar decisions to bring along their children, some not much older than Chloe, carrying American flags and NOT MY PRESIDENT signs. Alejandra was handed a NOT MY PRESIDENT sign, which as a lawful permanent resident unable to vote, she felt was true enough to hold aloft. For Chloe, we gave her a much simpler concept to champion: bundled in her jacketed arms was a LOVE TRUMPS HATE sign that outsized her. She had become caught up in the excitement, waving the sign around in her hands. It was her first protest and she took to it naturally.

Protest marches in New York have long been part of the city's blood, but when the shock of the election wore off, there seemed to be a citywide focused rage, and I wondered if it was spreading nationally. Instead of the social causes that rallied people without entirely unifying them, here we had one man, one name—Trump—and there was nothing to dispute. This march, immediately, within the first syllables of the first chant rhythmically accompanied by our footsteps on the pavement, felt like a unification. He represented every injustice and offered a focal point to jointly confront. No matter what one believed in, there was evidence that Trump was the antithesis of it. This unity, so visceral in a march, was powerful enough to make the worst of America—systemic racism, corporate greed, latent jingoism and nativism—seem defeatable. Ironically, under a Trump administration, there could be room for optimism, for a resistance we all agreed upon.

At Trump Tower, however, the march ceased, and our momentum and spirit had a physical target. Alejandra, caught up in the fervor of the crowd, shouted *"Hijo de Puta!"* at the tower, while I covered Chloe's ears. Trump's signature building is the color of coal and as shiny as a slick of oil. I'd never been inside to see its gilded interior, its three-story waterfall, or its panoply of high-end vendors, and now to do so, especially for those that lived there, would mean, at least for the foreseeable future, having to navigate inordinate security. I wondered if people were already planning to move out, to less controversial real estate. I knew he was there now, up in his penthouse, perhaps looking down on the crowd, or perhaps on the other side, already receiving the first of the procession of visitors who had come to kiss the small, jeweled hand of the newly crowned, lobby for a position in the cabinet, or try to grab his ear in the hopes of doing good. This was before Trump's egregious behavior would make headlines daily. He was, for a brief moment, a man in his ebony tower, and fifty-eight stories below, a powerful opposition was announcing its presence. How little did we know just how immediately we would all be called to arms again the moment he came down to be inaugurated and move to his new white home in the nation's capital.

The holidays that passed during Trump's period as president-elect felt joyless. It felt like there was nothing to be thankful for at Thanksgiving, that there was nothing to celebrate at Christmas, that there was no future to desire at New Year's. The only bright spot were the reports of corruption and Russian influence in the election, which I naively hoped might grow to such proportions as to keep Trump out of the White House before he ever entered it. My concern for the millions of immigrants in this country, however, was growing daily. Trump's disdain for this U.S. demographic was at the forefront of his platform, and his promise of a wall, that supposedly Mexico would pay for, was terrifyingly well-received at his rallies. There was also another group of people he had set his sights on—Muslims. He had been calling for a ban on foreign Muslims from entering the country, and condemned the San Bernardino and Pulse Nightclub shootings, while ignoring the overwhelming domestic terrorist attacks instigated by disgruntled Caucasians. To anyone who had been paying attention, it was all but certain that all people considered "foreign"—which seemed to have a rapidly broadening definition—would be among the first people that Trump, as president, would pounce upon.

Like I had done for the DACA/DAPA hearing nearly six months before, I set off on a bus full of immigration activists to Washington, DC for another galvanizing assembly. The "We Are Here to Stay" rally held only six days before Trump's inauguration, wasn't to be held on the streets, but at the historic Metropolitan African Methodist Episcopal Church, just a few blocks north of the White House. The church was a beacon of civil rights and justice in the heart of the nation's capital, a place where the echo of Frederick Douglass's booming voice urging protection for the nation's "humblest citizens" could still be heard. Dozens of organizations were sponsoring this event, including Make the Road New York, the group I had come down with, which didn't just offer legal aid to undocumented immigrants, but held community organization workshops and policy innovation lectures as well. The list of speakers was impressive—Congressman Luis Gutiérrez and Senator Chris Van Hollen, among the House and Senate's most outspoken immigration reformers; the Service Employees International Union (SEIU) president Mary Kay Henry; Planned Parenthood president Cecile Richards; and several organizers, including one young woman who had once been one of our clients. After being granted immigration relief, she turned right around and started helping the immigrant community, utilizing her knowledge of its rights, its paths to relief, and how to defend itself against ICE. I felt a shiver of pride seeing her take to the podium and lead a chant of "No justice, no peace" before the packed house.

Banners bearing the day's rallying cries—WE ARE HERE TO STAY; END DEPORTATIONS/END CRIMINALIZATION/END OUR PAIN!!!; TÚ, YO, TODOS SOMOS AMERICA—covered the banisters and were otherwise hung in abundance. I found the speeches stirring, sometimes heartbreaking, as speakers tried to grapple with the era that lay ahead. None of them, though, no matter the person, no matter the words, no matter the vocal strength, affected me more than the music did. Between speakers, some classic tune of solidarity performed by a handful of musical acts would fill the nave. But it was the Howard University Gospel Choir that carried me off into what I can only describe as a safe passage through troubled times. For six minutes, while the transcendent group performed "Hold On, Change Is Coming," I was lifted to a place I hadn't been to since November 8: the state of hope. It sounded exactly as I believed President Obama wanted hope to sound when he first shared that word and his vision for it during his first presidential campaign. Hope had come alive within me once again, an indescribable fulfillment of a rarely fulfilled sentiment. Hope went into each rhythmic clap, Hope spilled from the chorus:

Hold on,
change is coming,
hold on,
don't you worry about a thing,
hold on,
you can make it,
hold on,
everything will be alright.

And again. Over and over again. It felt, in the best way possible, eternal. It was not repetition because each word changed, grew in us and thus emerged from our voices in a new form. The words were a recognition and an assurance that none of us knew we needed but hungrily accepted, and which cracked open, momentarily, the hardened cocoon we had all been cultivating since the election. Time and Trump and the world were for later. *Hold on* was what mattered. The entire church knew this and sang it as such, gathering strength, each time like a breath of air before a deep plunge. When the choir came down off the stage and filled in the rows between pews, their blue and black robes rustling against us, it filled the space with an electrifying current. And while some in the crowd spoke no English, everyone helped carry that song along, for it contained a common language. *Hold on . . .* the repetition became a fortification, said enough times to believe it, to convince ourselves and someone or something other than ourselves that this was possible, that we would, indeed, hold on.

The song lingered as we filed onto the bus. On the bus ride back to New York City, I engaged in a lively debate with a young man from Queens who was a lawful permanent U.S. resident. He told me that he had recently become eligible for U.S. citizenship, but felt disinclined to apply.

"Why not?" I asked.

"Because the U.S. just elected a man that will start a war against immigrants," he said. "If I were to become a U.S. citizen, then I'd be 'agreeing to bear arms for the United States if the law requires it,' as the oath mandates, which means that I could be called upon to 'support and defend the Constitution and laws of the United States of America against all enemies,' and if those enemies are my people, then I'd be betraying them and their hopes of living here to uphold my newly acquired responsibility to do so."

He made an interesting case, but honoring it meant that he didn't have the protections that came with citizenship, including security against deportation. "Don't you think you'll need the rights and protections of citizenship with this incoming administration? And voting too—do you want Trump to get reelected in four years? Your vote means something," I naively concluded.

"Does it though?" He looked at me askance. "Even if I had become a citizen before this last election, Trump still would have won. You're right about deportation, and that's maybe the toughest benefit to ignore, especially now. But I think back to persecutions throughout history and wonder just how many people would have been saved from exile, or torture, or death if they had sworn off their beliefs and identities? That's how I see citizenship: an offer to give up myself in order to be given the rights of someone else. I don't want to swear fealty to a nation that won't take others just like me. Think of African Americans and women suffragettes, who, until they were granted formal citizenship on their own terms, were treated like second-class citizens—I mean, damn, they still are. And that's what I'd be if I became a citizen—second class—and that's no citizenship at all."

As the young man finished his thoughts, I thought of my mother, who became a citizen in 1979. What did she think about the oath she took? Was it the same oath? Would she take it again today? I had filled out dozens of N-400 naturalization applications, and I had never taken the oath seriously or really considered it. I felt it was similar to those long Terms of Service agreements used by companies like Apple, which pop onto your computer screen and you click "I Agree" after quickly skimming a few words in order to move on. The young man I spoke with made me consider the civil disobedience of his act and the fine print of the oath as a binding contract to thoroughly consider.

The bus moved slowly north as the weather grew worse. Snow began to pile up along the sides of the highway. Traffic began crawling and the trip stretched deeper into the night. It was past midnight when we arrived back in New York City. The buildings and sidewalks were dusted with white. Everything seemed different, though the changes were just beginning. The song we had all sung together earlier came back into my head as I trudged through the soft, fresh snow.

======

Two weeks later, the worst I had been anticipating ever since the election reared its head, just days after Trump's inauguration. The first Tuesday of his presidency, an email from the International Refugee Assistance Project made me sit up in my seat:

> Credible reports indicate that the Administration may place a hold on refugee resettlement this week, possibly as soon as Jan. 25th at 11 am. Each day, vulnerable refugees who have been accepted for U.S. resettlement board commercial flights for the United States. No matter when an executive order is signed, refugees who have already departed will lose their admissibility while they are mid-air.
>
> The airports where we anticipate needing attorneys (so far) over the next two days are *Newark, Washington-Dulles, JFK, LAX, O'Hare, and Miami.*

I couldn't believe what I was reading. People who had been granted refugee status were to be ordered deported as soon as they landed. Were it not for the call to arms—a very different call to arms than what the young man on the bus had spoken about—for attorneys like myself, I would have probably remained dumbfounded in my seat. Instead, I filled out the necessary information immediately, stating my availability for John F. Kennedy Airport (JFK) for as many days as needed.

Twenty-four hours later, two anti-immigrant executive orders had been signed, one that officially mandated that Trump's wall be built, five thousand more border patrol officers hired, and new detention centers built—without stating where the funding for these additions would come from—and another that gave vast new powers to ICE in its ability to detain and deport, while also tripling the number of ICE agents and making every immigrant with a criminal record, even those with a jaywalking ticket, an enforcement priority. All that day, phones rang off the hook and our waiting room filled with immigrants under various statuses frightened with how these new orders could impact their lives here in the United States. Meanwhile, I was stunned at how quickly this new administration was able to act on anti-immigration policy, something Obama had struggled for years to do on behalf of any pro-immigration policies. While I grappled with this mess, that afternoon another email, forwarded by a colleague, contained a link to a *Washington Post* article with a leaked draft of another executive order: *Protecting the Nation from Foreign Terrorist Entry into the United States.* This was the title to what would become popularly known as "the travel ban." As indicated in the text, "Foreign Terrorists" meant anyone and everyone from seven predominantly Muslim countries. Within the first sentences, the order invoked the terrorist attacks of September 11, 2001, as justification, suggesting that such a ban as was currently in draft form and soon to be executed would have saved the United States from these attacks. The leaked draft of the travel ban went on to state who should be kept out of the United States, which would seemingly include most, if not all, of those employed in the White House, from the president on down:

the United States should not admit those who engage in acts of bigotry or hatred (including "honor" killings, other forms of violence against women, or the persecution of those who practice religions different from their own) or those who would oppress Americans of any race, gender, or sexual orientation.

Many of the proclamations made in the order were infuriating:

Sec. 3. Suspension of Issuance of Visas and Other Immigration Benefits to Nationals of Countries of Particular Concern . . . I hereby proclaim that the immigrant and nonimmigrant entry into the United States of aliens from countries referred to in section 217(a)(12) of the INA, 8 U.S.C. 1187(a)(12), would be detrimental to the interests of the United States, and I hereby suspend entry into the United States, as immigrants and nonimmigrants, of such persons for 90 days from the date of this order . . .

if not outright inhumane:

Sec. 5. Realignment of the U.S. Refugee Admissions Program for Fiscal Year 2017 . . . (c) Pursuant to section 212(f) of the INA, 8 U.S.C. 1182(f), I hereby proclaim that the entry of nationals of Syria as refugees is detrimental to the interests of the United States and thus suspend any such entry until such time as I have determined that sufficient changes have been made to the USRAP to ensure that admission of Syrian refugees is consistent with the national interest.

The Syrian Civil War, then at its peak, was producing close to a dozen casualties a day, many of whom were civilians likely eligible for refugee status and asylum in the United States. Some had already been approved by the U.S. government and were already on their way, as were refugees from other war-torn nations, men and women persecuted for their religious beliefs, sexual orientation, and political views, who, like the Syrians, the United Nations had designated as refugees and the United States had accepted. With the signing of the travel ban, they would lose their refugee status to enter the United States in mid-air. Traumatized and uprooted, the hope they felt on boarding a flight to the United States of America would be snuffed out. They would be oblivious to all of this happening on the ground, though. Instead, they would be staring out the window at the Atlantic Ocean, waiting to see the lights of New York City coming into view, just as generations ago, immigrants on steamships headed for Ellis Island, would see the torch of Lady Liberty on the horizon, a plaque beneath her sandaled feet that stated her guardianship of the American Dream:

> *Your huddled masses yearning to breathe free,*
> *The wretched refuse of your teeming shore.*
> *Send these, the homeless, tempest-tost to me.*
> *I lift my lamp beside the golden door!*

As I boarded a train home on Friday afternoon, the travel ban officially went into effect. Attorneys were already headed to JFK, but I wasn't able to go immediately, so I was put on standby until further notice. No one knew what to expect—what the scene at JFK would be like, what orders had already been put into effect by TSA, or whether the order would be upheld for even a couple hours more.

The next morning, I was up early with Chloe, who always

slept until 9:00, but who that day woke us up at 6:00 a.m. I fed her a breakfast of mushed cereal and cut-up fruit, and as was our Saturday-morning ritual, we watched cartoons, while letting Alejandra sleep in. I briefly glanced at my emails during a commercial, and remnants of yesterday afternoon's bomb were scattered throughout my inbox. The call to arms I'd originally signed up for was now in full effect. All volunteer attorneys able to report to JFK's Terminal 4 should do so immediately. With some reluctance and much anxiety, I woke Alejandra. While I showered and dressed, she took over as master of the cartoon ceremonies. With a quick kiss to both I was out the door, a "Good luck!" following on my heels, as I rushed off to the Utica Avenue A train stop.

From the A, I switched over to a crowded AirTrain, JFK's airport-wide transit system. There were the usual travelers who kept their travel bags close as they held onto the steel rails of the train, patiently waiting to arrive at their terminal. I couldn't imagine any of them had a clue as to what was going down. And yet, I spotted a small group of warmly dressed people holding handmade signs and talking excitedly. I overheard one traveler ask them where they were headed, and when the woman from the group informed him of what had just transpired, the man took out his phone. I watched as he thumbed a few characters, his eyes widening only seconds later.

"Oh shit," he said. "Oh shit. Oh my god."

Other people, now curious, began making inquires as to what had so startled the man, nearly all of them sharing similar reactions. By the time I reached the terminal, the serenity of ignorance they had carried with them when they entered the train had vanished. They would be flying on what was likely the most notorious day in JFK's history.

Signs of chaos were palpable at Terminal 4. The lobby was

filled with people on phones, looking up at arrival boards with their hands gesticulating frustration. Behind a steel barrier, friends and family members waiting for loved ones at the doors where arrivals exited baggage claim and customs craned their necks each time someone walked through it. It was now close to 10:00 a.m., and police had set up a barricade with an already sizable crowd growing behind it. The frigid January air meant that protestors were making frequent use of bathrooms, and bringing back hot coffee from the café. This slowed traffic, which appeared jammed up all the way to the entrance of the terminal. Yet no one seemed to be honking, not out of aggression anyway, and I wondered (rightly, I would later discover) if these drivers, many of them from the countries Trump had banned, were on our side.

I made my way to the main arrivals board, where lawyers had been instructed to meet. Beyond the steel barrier, I spotted a group of people surrounded by laptops and cell phones. A TSA agent confirmed that that's where the lawyers and reporters were convening and that I could go through the barriers to get to them. When I tried to do so, I was halted by a cop who seemed particularly nervous, just as everyone around me seemed on edge. Despite explaining that I was volunteer lawyer, it was only when I showed him my credentials that he let me through. A woman named Michelle introduced herself as the shift coordinator, checked me in, and brought me up to speed. People were already detained at Terminals 1, 7, and 4, which was the lawyer and reporter headquarters. An adjacent café directly behind provided Wi-Fi, coffee, tables, and chairs.

"And how long is a shift?" I asked Michelle.

"You're volunteering," replied Michelle. "So it's up to you. We're hoping for at least a four-hour commitment, but we also have people who have been here since before the flights started coming in, pounding out *habeas corpus* petitions one by one. Same with the director who set this up. She's a machine that seems to run only on coffee."

I found an open space among a group of lawyers and got to work. Sitting next to me was a sixty-eight-year-old retired solo practitioner who spoke of immigration law in the Reagan 1980s, when she was just starting out. "Back then," she said adjusting the brim of her dusty hat, "even a Republican like Reagan was reasonable toward immigrants. Not like those sycophants in Congress who are genuflecting to Trump, rather than challenge an order like this. Even my arthritis wasn't enough to keep me from coming today!"

Next to her was a lawyer at a massive corporate law firm who just left the office at nine or ten the night before, trying to close a deal. "I have massive respect for human rights and immigration lawyers," he said. "Least I could do was come out and help." He stood up. "You guys need some coffee?" he asked. I gave him my order and he refused the five-dollar bill I tried to hand him. And that was generally the vibe: lawyers with powerful clients or employed at high-paying firms, but who knew next to nothing about immigration law, were willing to be translators, coffee runners, researchers, anything that was needed to optimize the amount of work we could do. And help from unlikely places continued to come. When authorities denied AirTrain entry to anyone without a boarding pass, one of the lawyers—or more likely, the press—must have gotten through to Governor Cuomo, because almost as soon as this requirement went into effect, it was also repealed. Uber, the controversial taxi-for-hire service, offered to foot the bills of all protestors needing a ride home.

That's when the protest really grew, taking the entire space between Terminal 4's doors and its parking garage, with some even ensconced within the parking garage itself—thousands of people warming each other in the cold, relentlessly holding up their homemade signs such as NEW YORK CITY STANDS WITH REFUGEES and BUILD BRIDGES, NOT WALLS until shoulders ached and their hands froze. The barricades groaned under the weight of the protest. TV vans raised their thirty-foot antennas. From time to time, a public official would speak or give an interview, seizing the moment and the momentum. Among the protesters, there was harmony in their outrage. Jews came to defend Muslims. Immigrants stood for other immigrants, for infinite future immigrants. There was a mix of anger and hope and righteousness. People who could remember such a time talked of the 1960s, and those who couldn't imagined it, feeling closer to a forgotten idealism. Everyone deplored the Executive Order signed yesterday at 4:39 p.m., and the man who signed it.

No Ban, No Wall!
No Ban, No Wall!
No Ban, No Wall!

Chants ricocheted from the metal beams of the JFK parking garage through to the smog of LAX, where a similar scene was unfolding, and airports in between. Breaths were frozen in the winter air, the words hanging in the cold. Both gloved and bare fists were held high, moving in unison with the four syllables of the chant. Voices were relentless and the resistance—to the weather, to weariness, to the president and his ideals—was contagious. People brought coffee and pizza and snacks and shared until there was none left, and then more arrived within minutes. American flags were hung on the metal barricades or held in the air. Posters of a woman wearing an American flag hijab were scattered among the crowd. Strangers hugged, held hands, and became allies and friends.

=====

I remained sheltered from the actual people this ban was affecting, that is until Michelle told us she had gotten word that there were people detained at Terminal 1. The scene there was much like Terminal 4, but with fewer protesters and the same number of bewildered travelers. Only this time, I wasn't seated with other lawyers, rather the coordinator here introduced me to a tall, slender Iranian man with ruffled black hair and two-day-old stubble.

"Mohammad," he said with agitation.

I asked him to explain his situation.

"I've already explained it to so many other people," he said, then momentarily closed his eyes. "I'm sorry. I drove all night from Columbus, Ohio, and haven't slept much since then. The fear of my wife's deportation to Iran is the only thing keeping me from going."

"I understand that this is all very maddening," I said. "But the more information I have the better I can help."

Mohammed took a deep breath and began to speak.

"I'm a third-year PhD candidate in biochemistry at the University of Ohio, where I live alone. But I am married, and after a grueling visa process, my wife who still lives in Iran finally got approved to join me here. She was supposed to fly into New York and then we would be driving back together. And then I found out that Trump had passed this ban, and that my wife would likely be turned away here in New York. I left straight from the lab to get here, listening to the most intense music I could find on the radio to stay awake. Other than my wife's flight info, which she forwarded to me, I didn't really have a plan, I just came straight to the airport, arriving at around 3:00 a.m. The guards told me that they didn't know anything about my wife's flight and that arrivals wouldn't start coming in for another three hours. They let me sleep here, though, and when I awoke, it was 8:00 a.m., and people were everywhere and I thought I had missed her. I was eventually directed to someone here who offered to find me legal help. I still don't really know what's happening."

I shared his sentiment. We talked for around thirty minutes, during which time he told me with tears in his eyes that his wife had called to tell him she was at the airport but would likely be sent back to Tehran. "She told me she loved me and that she hoped we would be together again soon." His emotional state caught the attention of a reporter who interrupted us and requested Mohammad for an interview. "As long as he can come with us," Mohammad said, nodding his head at me. I waited nearby while two cameramen setup in the parking lot, this one devoid of protesters, and Mohammad recollected to the anchor much of what he had just told me, and adding some questions about this country's integrity that were as true as they were likely to be cut from the broadcast.

I stayed with Mohammed, comforting him with the news that no one had yet been deported as far as I knew. He clung to this information like a lifeline, vowing not to leave until her fate had been confirmed. Then, around 5:00 p.m., his wife called him again, saying that the people were trying to force her to sign a document abandoning her status as a student visa derivative. I instructed Mohammad to translate between me and her.

"What are they telling her?"

"She says they're threatening to ban her from the U.S. if she doesn't cooperate and sign."

"They can't do that. Tell her not to sign anything, and to tell them that she has a lawyer willing to represent her immediately who is waiting in arrivals."

I didn't speak Persian, but I could hear a shift in his vocal tone from exasperated into something heart-wrenching and tender. Then he got off the phone. "I told her that if she is sent back that I will take the first flight home to be with her." It was a major decision, but Mohammad seemed to want nothing more to do with this country, and that he'd rather give his mind to a university in a more tolerable country, a powerful sentiment from an Iranian. Even still I gave Mohammed my card, which contained my cell phone number, and told him if he needed a place to stay tonight, to call me. He nodded and put the card in his pocket without much of a glance.

After I left Mohammed, I was introduced to another Iranian woman whose mother had been detained, likely on the same flight as Mohammad's wife. "My mother is seventy years old," she told me, "she's a housewife, not a terrorist." She too hadn't heard of the travel ban until she had arrived at the airport. In her hand were flowers that had already begun to droop dryly from the artificial heating. The arrival doors opened up and, like every other person here waiting for a miracle, the woman deadlocked her eyes on the people emerging from them. Her mother was not among them. I overheard an elderly Japanese woman walking past us tell a younger Caucasian girl: "I think I got off the plane into 1945." I knew what she meant. A Yemeni medical student at Stony Brook, returning from a family holiday was held despite his credentials, as was a Sudanese national who had no family and we weren't allowed to speak with. Not being able to communicate with the detainees also meant that it was impossible to know the number of people being detained. Some said a dozen, others said a hundred or so. The immigration officials wouldn't confirm or deny anything. So many lawyers, including myself, did as the protestors did and made signs, hoping to draw the attention of family members waiting in the arrivals area: IMMIGRATION LAWYERS, HERE TO HELP.

Michelle, when I saw her again at Terminal 4, explained that legal representatives for the ACLU had managed to file with a federal judge in Brooklyn an Emergency Motion of Stay of Removal on behalf of two Iraqis detained at JFK. Both of these men had once worked at their own risk as interpreters for the U.S. military and, at least as far as American conflicts are concerned, should have been welcomed to the country as heroes. But it wasn't until around 9:00 p.m. that a federal judge in Brooklyn—Judge Ann M. Donnelly—had indeed received such a motion from the ACLU and granted it along with an injunction. Connelly's written response had been sent to my email, and her statement, after a long day of incertitude, was a much-needed tangible victory. I looked at the case heading, where the names of those two Iraqis were listed as going against, or "versus," the most powerful men in the world—and winning. The words SO ORDERED appeared like a big galvanizing FUCK YOU to Trump.

UNITED STATES DISTRICT COURT EASTERN
DISTRICT OF NEW YORK
DECISION AND ORDER
HAMEED KHALID DARWEESH and HAIDER
SAMEER ABDULKHALEQ ALSHAWI, on behalf of
themselves and others similarly situated,
Petitioners,

– against –
DONALD TRUMP, President of the United States;
U.S. DEPARTMENT OF HOMELAND SECURITY
("DHS"); U.S. CUSTOMS AND BORDER
PROTECTION ("CBP"); JOHN KELLY, Secretary of
DHS; KEVIN K. MCALEENAN, Acting Commissioner
of CBP; JAMES T. MADDEN, New York Field
Director, CBP,
Respondents.
ANN DONNELLY, District Judge.

[...]

WHEREFORE, IT IS HEREBY ORDERED that the respondents, their officers, agents, servants, employees, attorneys, and all members and persons acting in concert or participation with them, from the date of this Order, are

ENJOINED AND RESTRAINED from, in any manner or by any means, removing individuals with refugee applications approved by U.S. Citizenship and Immigration Services as part of the U.S. Refugee Admissions Program, holders of valid immigrant and non-immigrant visas, and other individuals from Iraq, Syria, Iran, Sudan, Libya, Somalia, and Yemen legally authorized to enter the United States.

IT IS FURTHER ORDERED that to assure compliance with the Court's order, the Court directs service of this Order upon the United States Marshal for the Eastern District of New York, and further directs the United States Marshals Service to take those actions deemed necessary to enforce the provisions and prohibitions set forth in this Order.

SO ORDERED.
Ann M. Donnelly
United States District Judge

Her statement didn't just save two men, it was worded to declare the entire travel ban illegitmate. All planned deportations were immediately halted. Cheers from other lawyers began to erupt around me, as if our favorite basketball team had just sunk a buzzer-beating, game-winning shot. The news was spreading so quickly and with such raucousness that the sound of planes departing and arriving was drowned out by the cheering of the protestors, the honking cabbies, and the applause from every-one inside. I was exhilarated and shouted until I was hoarse. It wasn't over, of course—the detainees hadn't been authorized for release, but the fight to do so now had much-needed federal mus-cle. More lawyers were coming in to take up overnight shifts, and I was heartened to see that the chain of legal support would continue unbroken for the detainees until that ultimate victory could be achieved and these people could be reunited with their families and welcomed into the country. I hoped they could hear our cries of joy, and that their spirits—as well as the spirits of those who waited outside the security gates, hoping and praying for them to pass through the arrivals door—were lifted by this promising development.

My daughter was already asleep when I got home that night, but Alejandra had stayed up to greet me. I told her in exten-sive detail about what I had just experienced until her eyes grew droopy. I too was exhausted, but I lay wide-eyed beside Alejan-dra. Something felt unresolved. I mentally flipped through my entire day, everything I had seen and met. Then I remembered Mohammed, and it clicked that I was still concerned about his whereabouts and the fate of his wife. Surely, he remained at JFK and had heard the news. Because I had given him my card, we did not exchange numbers and there was no way to contact him. I felt guilty about being able to come home to my wife in a way that he wasn't yet able to, but I knew he wouldn't be alone, that the overnight shift was there to help. I picked up my phone from the nightstand, scrolling through the email updates that continued to come in. I signed up for another shift at JFK, then put my phone down for the night and tried to sleep, though the contagious spirit of the day kept pulsating within me.

———

That the travel ban would be the first fight of so many to come came as no surprise to me. When his original travel ban was shot down, Trump just issued a new one only two months later, with some slight revisions that would allow Iraqi nationals and pre-approved Syrian refugees to enter the country. That too was shot down by a federal judge, this time in Hawaii. That June, the Supreme Court allowed for "a partial ban" to be put into place, and on the heels of that victory, the policy changes, rule shifts, and new protocols were issued seemingly weekly, some surreptitiously and others to great fanfare. Representing individuals in their immigration cases felt more and more like placing a Band-Aid on a hemorrhaging wound, and we were rapidly run out of Band-Aids. The hours became longer and, no matter the effort, the results less favorable.

At the same time, Alejandra and I were faced with a dilemma. Back in October 2016, when I was confident that we would not have the president we have, I had applied for a Fulbright to carry out research on unaccompanied minors crossing the Mediterranean and arriving in southern Spain. Alejandra was homesick, and we agreed a year in Spain would be good for us as a family, to live a different pace of life and be close to her family. And so I wrote a project proposal, got the letters of recommendation, and sent out the application. Then I forgot about it. Somewhere between court dates and the overwhelming workload now untenable in the early stages of the new Trump administration, I received an email that said I was a finalist and promptly forgot about that as well. But consciously I knew, if my luck carried, I would be faced with a predicament I am still grappling with. In April 2017, three months into the Trump presidency, I received an email congratulating me: the project I had written had been selected for funding. I had two weeks to accept or decline.

I struggled to share in the euphoria that Alejandra felt. Though I told myself repeatedly that this wouldn't be quitting, just a break from representing immigrants as their immigration lawyer, the deeper issue was the timing. This was, without a doubt, the worst time to leave the United States as an immigration lawyer, and things were clearly going to get much worse in the coming year. And yet, I was only spending an hour, or two at most, each day with Chloe; Alejandra's new job had her commuting an hour each way to the Bronx; both Alejandra's parents and mine were five-hour flights away, unable to help us with Chloe; and we were barely covering our expenses with two non-profit salaries in one of the most expensive cities in the world. I knew what the right decision was for us as a family, but I still fought hard to imagine myself away from this immigration war.

My last day at the organization was full of tears and hugs, but once everyone left for the weekend, I stayed behind after the office had closed, to finish a response to one client's Notice of

Intent to Deny (NOID)—a statement issued by the government to an applicant they feel does not qualify for relief. This NOID response felt scripted, as if these past two years in New York City were being summed up in these twenty pages I have written. The Clash's version of "I Fought the Law" was playing on repeat in the background noise of my mind, as it had been for the past few months. The setting sun cast the Statue of Liberty in an evening glow. The day had been unnaturally warm, the East River and Manhattan appearing calmer than usual. A slight breeze and a waning moon had already risen. I placed the finishing touches on the NOID response, and began writing personal notes to leave on each of my co-workers' desks.

All week, I had been packing my belongings and bringing them home—the only things left were the many quotes and Xeroxed pages from writers and their works that I had pinned onto the wall in front of my desk. Among them a passage from "On Not Going Home," a seminal essay by the literary critic and novelist James Wood, in which he used a word—afterwardness—repurposed from Freud and which, as Wood defined it, encompassed how I've always felt while working with immigrant youth.

> To think about home and the departure from home, about not going home and no longer feeling able to go home, is to be filled with a remarkable sense of "afterwardness": it is too late to do anything about it now, and too late to know what should have been done.

Just below a picture of Alejandra and Chloe sitting on the stoop at our building on Jefferson Avenue was another quote, this one by Che Guevara: *Hay que endurecerse sin perder jamás la ter-*

nura. I had originally put it up to offer the immigrant youth a road map, to harden themselves since they were both immigrants up against an unkind system and also youths who should hold on to their tenderness, since they deserved their innocence and childhoods. But over time, I had come to a better understanding of what that quote meant for me. By circumstance, these young people had experienced a journey that had already hardened them, and yet this tenderness never left them—though sometimes it had been scraped to the bone. If anything, it allowed them to remain hopeful and brave. I read it now as if Guevara was not theorizing on traits of the revolutionary but foretelling the fate of the immigrant youth in the United States.

A quote by the essayist Rebecca Solnit furthered this thought: *Resistance is first of all a matter of principle and a way to live, to make yourself one small republic of unconquered spirit.* And like the Guevara quote, the meaning of her words had evolved for me since I had first pinned them to the wall nearly two years before. When I was starting out, I thought of myself as part of a resistance, and that my career was a clear enunciation of this statement. Rereading it that night as I unpinned it, I knew that with resistance comes the tyranny and suffering it challenges— in other words, that I have not lived the resistance, but rather learned it. I have learned it from those who have resisted tyranny and suffering and pain that I cannot imagine. The unconquered spirit Solnit speaks of is that of the immigrant; that is their unquestionable identity, that is my mother, Alejandra, and the many immigrant youth I have had the honor to work with as their immigration lawyer. They are the true resistance, they are the ones I would keep in mind even as I closed the filing cabinet drawer to their case files for the last time.

I assembled all of my notes and history on the NOID case

and left it in a manila folder on Angie's desk, a sharp lawyer who would be taking over the case and filing the response for us on Monday. On the top I slapped on a Post-it with a short message: *You've got this*. And then I took the last box of my possessions and walked out the door into the incoming dusk of the evening. Sunset Park had never so beautifully lived up to its name.

PART V

_____

EXODUS

. . . .

You broke the ocean in half to be here, only to
meet nothing that wants you.

—*Nayyirah Waheed*

The exit row on the flight was empty. I moved to the front of the small propeller plane, which seemed to shift slightly with my movements. The exit row was made up of four seats facing one another. I took one of the seats that faced backward, so that as we left the Spanish mainland and flew south, I saw the Iberian Peninsula slowly recede. Below us, the Mediterranean looked more like a lake. The calm blue was being dissected by white wakes from boats traveling west toward the Strait of Gibraltar and east, farther into the Mediterranean. I strained my eyes and saw one white wake from a smaller boat traveling north. I found myself wondering if this was perhaps a boat full of migrants, making the deadly crossing to arrive in southern Spain and thus, Europe.

I switched seats ten minutes later. Now, I was facing forward, looking south, with Europe at my back. I could see the African continent looming before us. The propeller plane dipped and shook with the wind as the barren, rocky coast of Morocco came into view. The pilot banked left at a slender peninsula and we began to travel parallel to the coast. From my view on the right side of the plane, I saw that the Mediterranean was not, in fact, as calm as I imagined. The waves arrived in short quick bursts against the coastline, and what was once blue was now a foamy white with the aftershocks of the crashing waves.

My flight from Madrid to Melilla, a Spanish-owned city that dents the Moroccan coastline, was less than two hours long. Square cement houses dotted the dry hillsides, then suddenly a fence appeared and hundreds of buildings soon thereafter. Within a second, Morocco was gone. Without leaving the continent of Africa, we had returned to Europe.

The Mediterranean is pocked with such enclaves like Melilla, little geographic trophies held by Spain and the U.K. But while the U.K. territory of Gibraltar is perhaps the most famous, Melilla and Ceuta, two Spanish autonomous cities on the African mainland, and the only borders between Africa and Europe, are becoming the most notorious. Because it encompasses a larger land area, for many African migrants and refugees seeking to cross into Europe, Melilla is the front gate. And it's a hell of a gate: three, two-story chain-link fences equipped with razor and barbed wire in some areas and motion-sensitive alarms to alert the guards that patrol it twenty-four hours a day would have to be traversed just to make it to the overcrowded migrant reception center where refugees are processed for possible asylum. Melilla is compact enough that the fences inch right up to the city's shopping mall, some of its public parks, and most infamously a golf course, where, in 2014, a migrant activist and photographer named José Palazón took a photo of a group of African migrants straddling the fence, looking down at two golfers taking swings on a tee box below them. Palazón captioned the photo: "Immigrants on the fence, expulsions and a game of golf. Only in Melilla."

When the time came for me to make a research trip to Melilla, an advocate I had met in Granada put me in contact with

José. When I arrived in Melilla, I explained to José what I was doing here, and asked if he'd be up for grabbing a coffee. He quickly wrote back: "Absolutely."

During my flight, I had read a long article on Melilla's ongoing refugee crisis, stopping at a phrase used by Gianfranco Tripodo, a photojournalist who shot many of the spreads in the piece. Though other people were quoted at length, with one quip Tripodo gave a perfect description of the city, calling it "the border of the border." I reflected on this as I stepped outside the airport and into a fog of thick and saturating heat that soon layered my body in a coat of sweat. In the taxi queue were five white Mercedes from the early 1990s, looking like some former African dictator's entourage forced to find new work after he had been disposed. During my stay here I would see members of this ivory fleet darting through the old city's narrow streets and along the small highways that bordered the fence. I stepped inside of one and the driver asked in Spanish for my destination. Once he was speeding off toward it, however, he switched to Riffian Berber which he spoke into the cell phone clamped onto his dashboard. Behind us was the mountainous terrain of Morocco, rising above like a wave posed to crash upon the colonial holdout.

Melilla at first glance appeared charming. From the airport, I had a panorama of the city, a romantic vista that filled the eyes with the turquoise waters of La Cabo de Tres Forcas crashing upon the ramparts of the fortress that made up Melilla la Vieja, the large fortress to the north of the port. From its walls, a row of fishermen cast their lines. Cafés fronted characteristic and sandy-colored seaside architecture of the town center. Perhaps, I imagined naively, the school day had just finished— bands of children huddled in nooks at every turn, though none had backpacks or school supplies. People of older generations liberally crossed the smooth concrete streets, which were mostly absent of streetlights. The city was technically European, but it felt like the final remnant of Moorish Spain, outliving history, but emerging into modern times in a blend of burqas and Zara business suits, halal meats and *jamon serrano,* mint tea and *café con leche*, mosques and churches. In New York City, no one would have thought twice about this cultural hybrid, but here it was jarring. That is because Melilla is also Spanish beyond measure, even stubbornly so. It was a key staging ground for the launch of General Franco's rebellion in July 1936, and memories of the Fascist era dot the city. In Madrid, there is fierce debate about what to do with General Franco's remains, but in Melilla, the last statue of General Franco in a public area stands proudly, not far from Melilla La Vieja.

José had given me directions to a café that was near the old part of town. I still managed to get somewhat lost in the haphazard splintering of the old town's unlabeled corridors, and twice had to ask for directions. José was amicable about it, greeting me warmly as I offered my apologies. "You are right on time in Spanish time," he said in a gently accented Spanish, "I'm the one that got here too early." José had the worn, sun-beaten look of a *campesino*, a picture completed by his faded jeans and flannel shirt, his closely cropped hair paired with a long, speckled beard. He reminded me of a cousin who worked on a Chilean vineyard, and the familiarity immediately put me at ease. But José exuded the vitality and moral outrage of youth, a power he let burn slowly, like the cigarettes he smoked at our outdoor table, but one that kept us in conversation for hours.

The heat had not let up, yet we ordered two *cafés con leche* that arrived steaming in their cups. Unaccustomed to such twofold heat, I ordered a cup of ice to pour the hot liquid into. José asked about my work as an immigration lawyer, and was curious to hear my stories of working at the border. He was the first person I'd spoken with in Spain who, as a witness to such horrific scenes at the border here, was not shocked by what was happening in Trump's America, at least not at first. When I turned the conversation to him, asking about what it was like to live in a true border town, he paused to sip from his coffee, then responded broadly, indicting the treatment of migrants and their former homes generally. "We live well because they live badly," he said, placing the cup back on the table. José's phrasing in Spanish had the solemnity of an aphorism. *Nosotros vivimos bien porque ellos viven mal.* It was clear he had thought of this often but had never condensed his thoughts in this manner. He repeated it again, holding *bien* and *mal* for an extra beat, emphasizing the vast gulf he wished to convey. He continued, with an uncomplicated assurance, "Melilla is living a dichotomy, yet everyone here is an immigrant."

José was a permanent resident of Melilla, having lived in the city for the past thirty years after leaving the Spanish mainland. There were other Spaniards like him, he told me, who had come to call this European outpost home, the difference between here and a normal city being its transitory nature, a port town with people as its primary export. Everyone's considerations, it seemed, were toward what lay beyond the sea. It was as if Melilla were a wayward Spanish ship run aground in Morocco, with the crew trying to maintain order, its passengers establishing relations with the locals, and all the while stowaways attempting to climb aboard. Morocco, José went on, played its own role in managing Melilla's refugees. He described an unofficial agreement, similar to the agreement between the United States and Mexico to defend the Mexican–Guatemalan border, where Morocco is in essence the true gatekeeper of who gets admitted and denied entry into Melilla, sometimes employing brutal tactics to do so. While Syrian refugees were nearly always admitted, sub-Saharan African refugees for instance, were just as often barred from entry. "You won't find a Syrian trying to climb the fence," as José put it. Though Melilla had for generations been a destination for asylum seekers, it was only in 2014, in the midst of the Syrian Civil War, that Melilla opened an official asylum office. José described Syrians as "white" refugees, having the privilege to apply for and receive asylum a thousand times over. Conversely, José noted how during the same period, no African or "black" refugees had—at least to his knowledge—been granted asylum. "It's classic racial profiling," José said, "and even if this weren't the case, it is Syrians, not Africans, who can afford to bribe border guards."

This need often arises. Morocco has been known to limit the number of refugees that enter Melilla each day, which is not protocol officially mandated by Spain. If a hundred Syrians arrived at the Moroccan–Spanish border seeking asylum, Morocco might only let in a few at one time and tell the rest to come back tomorrow, even though Syrians are technically eligible for asylum and immediate entry. Morocco has traditionally been in control of the faucet, letting it drip slowly, but never letting the water flow freely. What complicates this relationship isn't Morocco or Spain, however—though the shifting politics of each often does—but Melilla itself, caught, quite literally, in between the two. In 2015, the city nearly collapsed under the weight of arriving Syrian refugees, which numbered close to fifty each day. From what I've been able to ascertain, most Syrians fleeing the Civil War followed a route that involved traveling to Turkey by road, where they would link up with a clandestine operation that promised to get them to Europe—this often meant Melilla. As part of the route, Syrians would fly directly to Algeria, which did not require visas for Syrian arrivals for a time, where smugglers would then escort them straight to a Melillan or Ceutan checkpoint and where the bribe would be paid to border security guards. This bribe was necessary because the Spanish asylum office is on Spanish soil; in other words, they cannot apply for asylum in Spain because they cannot enter Spain until they have the money to bribe Moroccan officials, as José succinctly puts it. While they wait to be processed, many Syrians have been subjected to robberies and assaults by gangs that have established a foothold in Melilla, since they are known to carry their entire life savings with them on their person, like walking, unarmed banks. Despite the constant business of immigration and the private luxury establishments that have popped up, Melilla remains a relatively poor city.

José remained convinced of the unspoken manifestation of colonialism into privatized capitalism, which diverts the massive resources and wealth away from sub-Saharan African nations and into the pockets of corporations, Western nations, and even political leaders of these same countries. In Equatorial Guinea, for instance, which has a booming oil industry and is among the wealthiest African nations, nearly all of its GDP ends up in the pockets of its president and ministers while the rest of the country is subjected to among the worst human rights violations on the planet. One exiled Equatorial Guinean writer named Juan Tomás Avila Laurel published *The Gurugu Pledge*, a haunting novel concerning a group of sub-Saharan migrants attempting to cross into Spain via Melilla to escape the horrors of their home. The title takes its name from one of the mountains that looms over Melilla. In the book, Avila Laurel echoes what José has told me. One of the characters states: "Don't ask me where I came from. It was via lots of places, but I came in through Algeria. They told me I no longer have a country, that's what they said at the border: you've no country anymore, now you're just black."

José believes that the solution—if such a thing exists—to the current migration crisis is a reverse deportation. By our second *café con leche*, he became more animated, leaning forward across the table and using hand gestures every few words. "Deport the corporations, the heavy-handed diplomats, even the NGOs," José told me, his shoulders shrugged and his hands raised, like I had seen my father-in-law and most Spaniards do. "That way, this process of billion-dollar mines owned and controlled by foreign corporations, of coffee and sugar plantations sold at free-trade prices, of misappropriated aid from NGOs, of oil flowing to the West, revenue that returns only to the pockets of corrupt leaders of starved and bare African and Latin American nations, will finally be put to an end."

"Even the NGOs?" I asked, a bit intimidated by José's convictions.

"Absolutely. In the poorest countries, NGOs and the UN have large, sleek offices, with photos of starving African children on their walls and have more say in the local government than the residents. And those children, they often end up in the worst situations, even if they do manage to make it here."

To prove his point, he gestured at the beach that edged the foundational walls of the fortress, where teenage boys swam in the modest waves of the Mediterranean, at the same moment that most youth their age were in school. Over their laughter, someone shouted something to them in what José identified as Riffian Berber. "You see those kids?" he asked, nodding his head in their direction. "They're immigrants too, existing like families of stray cats," he said, fondly. "They're survivors. Some have parents, some don't. But all of them are here alone." I looked down toward the water and saw a vision of the youth I worked with in New York City. "They're not even allowed to

attend school or work, though some shine shoes or try working on their own, however they can. Until they are registered
with the police, they are not even considered to exist here. But
they also can't be deported, not until they are eighteen. It's
why they roam without a purpose. And the years just pass,
without any education or learning any meaningful skills. They
get older and one day, two or three years later, they are eighteen and deported from Melilla. It's a waste of time, a waste
of effort by the Spanish government, and these kids who have
so much to give. You should hear some of the things they tell
me. Half of them dream of playing *fútbol* for Madrid or Barcelona." He smiles to himself, then shakes his head slightly.
"Other than each other, they really have nobody but a couple
of overcrowded shelters and the occasional advocate to speak
on their behalf."

Even before arriving in Melilla, I knew that among their biggest champions was José himself. This has only been affirmed
from everything I've seen during my time here. Though he is an
outspoken activist, José is a humble person in private conversation. Several weeks later, while reading Spain's most widely
read newspaper, *El País*, I came across a spread of him and
eleven *menores extranjeros* (unaccompanied minors) ages five
to eighteen, protesting in front of a government building for the
opportunity to attend school.

And like a saint, José provides more than he keeps. He is
the rare activist with no ego, no ulterior motive. To the young
migrants who arrive in Melilla, he is unofficially a lawyer, a
psychologist, a cook, and everything in between. Every Tuesday night, for example, he leads a group of volunteers into the
abandoned buildings and caves by the sea with platters of food
and eats with the immigrant youth living in these places. While
he makes a living as a private tutor teaching private classes and

offering tutoring to college students taking Spain's dreaded public service exams, José spends the rest of the time being a father
figure to many fatherless boys.

We swapped stories about working at centers for migrant
children, finding the similarities and differences between how
things worked here and back in the United States. There were
two youth centers in Melilla, one with a good reputation for how
they treat the *menores* who stay there, and one that is dreaded,
according to José. "Most of the young people you see on the
streets," José said, "likely couldn't get into the better center,
which is small and always crowded. They are sent to the other
bigger center," which José described as being much more rigid
than its counterpart. I thought of the youth at the Karnes Detention Center and could only wonder how "rigid" he meant. Both
centers, however, have open-door policies: the young people that
live there were free to come and go as they pleased. I was aston-
ished by this. "They're not jails," José assured me, "but places to
receive young people when they first arrive, reception centers."
The name brought to mind the farcical "residential centers"
that dot the United States and where no resident is allowed to
leave, unless a judge or the government grants permission after
a lengthy process.

"That's not how things are done in the U.S.," I said. "Reception centers there are like prisons. Many youth in the U.S. do
end up leaving sooner though: after months in these prisonlike
places, they will sign deportation orders just to get out."

"And what about Trump?" he asks, the question that has
most defined my time in Spain and interactions with Spaniards.
"How much worse has it become during his presidency? I've
been hearing about parents being separated from their children."

His question reflected the headlines in every major newspaper, even in Spain. Not only did the news of child separation

break that week, but the depth of how bad the situation was seemed to have no end. I had spoken to colleagues along the border who were still in shock and couldn't even explain to me, fully, what was happening.

"It's awful. They are separating parents from their children, telling the parents they're taking the kids for a bath or a doctor's visit and then never returning them. I've heard that some of the parents have already been deported without their children. They are even keeping some of the children in cages, with nothing but these emergency thermal blankets."

"Cages?"

"Yes, cages."

I pulled up an article showing children being housed in groups within a chain-link fenced cage within a windowless gymnasium, which made José's eyes go wide.

"Horrible," said José, holding his forehead with his fingertips. "No one should jail children, and of course never put them in cages. Maybe an open-door policy like we have here is an impossibility, but something like a curfew or check-in system would be so much more humane. I don't think it is a good idea to let children roam on their own either. Some of the kids walk out of the center at night, and the next morning we might hear that they've been arrested or hospitalized from a bad beating, or they just disappear."

I could see his point, but the current state of affairs far surpassed any rational discussion of what was and wasn't a good idea. I explained to José the nuances of Trump's derided and detested "zero-tolerance" policy, enacted that April, though reportedly "tested out" as early as October of the previous year, and which included the cages. "If a family or a parent and their child try to cross the border, the parents will get prosecuted for the federal crime of illegal entry and they will throw the parents into federal prison, while sending the kids to shelters, or else locking them up in cages. The kids are then treated, under the law, as unaccompanied minors, as if they arrived alone. These kids obviously haven't, but by initiating this chain of events and deporting parents alone, the kids eventually are unaccompanied minors because of the government's actions. Or orphans, really." I told him how the U.S. border was becoming similar to Melilla's as well. "There are people lining up at the border checkpoints, trying to apply for asylum, but the border officials won't let them. They tell them that they aren't processing applicants that day. People end up sleeping on the bridges, setting up camps around the checkpoints. Most will finally give up and try to cross the border somewhere else. That's when they'll get picked up for 'illegally' crossing and get separated from their children." The "zero-tolerance" policy would eventually be halted by litigation and repealed by an Executive Order, but only after so many people, including some of Trump's own supporters, protested it. Even after the executive order, however, friends and advocates along the border still reported separated families. Before all that happened, nearly three thousand children would be affected, many not recognizing their own parents when reunited later in the summer. Many would never be reunited with their parents, becoming orphaned by a policy that hoped to deter future immigrants. At the time, as I told José all of this, I felt like a soldier on leave right when his battalion deployed. The immigration war in the United States was heading into one of its darkest hours, and I was for the most part absent.

"I feel guilty being here and not there, to help," I said finally, after explaining the current policy and its effects as I understood them.

José nodded patiently.

"And what do you hope to learn here in Europe?" he said, emphasizing *Europa* with a hint of irony.

"I guess if there is something from your system that would help us to improve ours."

José thumbed his beard, momentarily lost in thought. "Every system," he said, "can be improved. It is not perfect here. At this border, there is probably more police violence than any other border you'll see. Don't take that back with you to the U.S. At the very least, tell them to treat children like children."

On the walk back to my hotel, José points out the place where dozens of migrant children live, a barren concrete building with holes instead of windows. José glanced at his watch. "11:15 a.m.," he said, "they're waking up now. They will start going to *el rastro*, a street market here in town, soon. I am late for another appointment, but if you go now, you will see them begging or attempting to steal a lunch. If you want to do something for them, buy fruit and bread and offer that to the group. They'll appreciate it, I'm sure."

As we shook hands goodbye, he asked when I'd be making my way toward the CETI. "Sometime this afternoon," I said. He nodded. "Take cigarettes with you. There's nowhere to buy them out there, and even if there was, they have no money. It's an easy way to make friends and get people talking." And with that, he walked off down the street.

———

The CETI was the *Centro de Estancia Temporal de Inmigrantes* (the Center for Temporary Stay for Immigrants) a monolithic complex made up of dozens of barracks located across the highway from Melilla's golf course and just over the bridge from a dried-up riverbed. Clouds of dust plumed from the cab's tires as we sped toward the road that led to it. It bordered the city limits, made undoubtable by the fences that were in full view. The houses of Farkhana were visible immediately beyond the fence. The cab pulled into a parking lot and into what seemed like an encampment. Loud music was blasting out of speakers; two men sat on a weather-beaten couch, hidden behind cardboard walls, nodding along. Nearby was a fire pit, which showed signs of recent use, accompanied by two large rocks used as chairs. A lone man was seated there, his eyes locked on me as I made my way toward him. I greeted him in Spanish.

"*No hablo, no hablo*," said the man waving me off.

Remembering José's advice, I pulled out the pack of cigarettes and offered one to him. He took one and nodded in gratitude, then rubbed his thumb across his forefinger, the universal gesture for a light. I reached into my back pocket and pulled out the neon green lighter that I had bought with the pack. I cupped the small flame and brought it toward the cigarette in his mouth. He took a deep drag. With his other hand, the man touched his heart.

"*Ayat*," he said. "*Tú?*"

I mimicked his movement. "Jon."

I had stopped trying to explain "J. J." to anyone in Spain. He spoke my name to himself a few times, as if he had never heard a name that I always assumed was common. Ayat looked young and I felt guilty for giving him a cigarette. I tried to ask for directions to the main office, but our ad hoc hand gestures weren't well understood. He finally got up, and with a brief smile, headed toward the men on the couch. I headed in the opposite direction, toward some faded yellow buildings with flat, dark orange roofs, surrounded by a tall and thick metal fence around their perimeter. It appeared to be a sort of shantytown, with people walking about washing clothes in a basin area and hanging their wet clothes on laundry lines clipped at one end to the thick fence encompassing the CETI. Again I tried to speak with people, asking a group of young men *"Español?* English?" They shook their heads, and when I shoved the packet of cigarettes through the opening in the fence and offered a cigarette, they shook them again.

What I didn't see were guards. At the wide-mouth entrance of the CETI, there was a small building, which looked more like a tollbooth and one guard worked there, as the migrants swiped their cards to get in and out at a turnstile. Another guard stood nearby lifting the manual barrier arm when cars approached. This guard told me that I couldn't get into the CETI without government authorization. Still, security here was much more minimal than I had anticipated. From what I could tell, this was not a detention center, but something more like a halfway house. But I needed a guide if I were to do much more than trace the perimeter. And just then, I heard an *hola*?

An older man with kind eyes and a taut leather face was approaching me carrying a satchel stuffed with baguettes under his arm. He repeated his greeting, as if to test my friendliness. I responded in kind, and gently tested his language abilities by asking if he was a resident of the CETI.

"Yes, I live here," he said in basic but sturdy Spanish. "Are you looking for someone?"

He had a spirited and friendly voice, though it was laced with exhaustion.

"I'm a reporter," I said, giving him a white lie. I wasn't sure what other reason I could give him for being here. "I am looking for someone to show me around the CETI."

He grips my hand firmly and shakes it. "I am Omar. I am from Algeria, but I have lived in Nador for many years before coming here. What is your name?"

"My name is Jon," I said. As I had previously done, I took out the pack of cigarettes and offered Omar one, which he took without hesitation. I handed him the lighter and he quickly sparked it.

"Jon, so English."

"American."

Omar lets out a raspy laugh at the mention of this. "What brings an American to the CETI? Are you lost? Or scouting for a new military base maybe?"

"No," I said, slightly embarrassed. "I'm reporting on immigration issues here and the comparison with the American–Mexican border."

Omar nods. "I spoke with another reporter a few months ago. He didn't think there was a story here. He wanted to find migrants that were trying to get on boats and cross the Mediterranean. That's the big story I guess."

Omar took another drag.

"I will show you this place, the real place though," he said, abruptly. "Come, I have to deliver some bread."

As we began to walk, he explained how he lived in Beni Ansar for a time, the town right outside the gates, waiting for his chance to enter Melilla. "If you are from Beni Ansar," Omar said, "you get a pass to come into the city. Many of the maids that clean the hotels or nanny children here, that's where they come from." Every morning Omar came with a bag of day-old food provided by the sympathetic owner of a café, who would have otherwise discarded it. He walked the three or so miles into town each day to pick it up, his sandals nearly worn through. While he claimed that it was for the people in the barracks, I followed him past the buildings and down the steep walls of the riverbed. A patch of tall foliage blocked our path, but Omar brushed it aside, letting me enter first and then letting the flora fall back into place. For a moment, we were completely hidden from view, and I started to get anxious. I had everything on me—camera, wallet, phone— and Omar needed only to brandish a knife to rob me. I kept walking, however, and before I could fully panic, Omar pulled aside another knob of growth and into view came homemade tents roofed by cardboard, plastic bags, and strands of the foliage, with torn blankets and pillows beneath them. Here he distributed the bread, including laying a loaf next to a man sleeping shirtless in the oppressive heat.

"These are people whose CETI permit has expired, or who the guards have kicked out of the CETI but have nowhere else to go. Morocco doesn't want them, and so they stay hidden on the outskirts."

As Omar took us back on a path away from the makeshift village and back toward the parking lot, I asked him questions about life in the CETI.

"It is not easy," he told me, "as you can see, even a loaf of bread can come as a gift. The CETI is a strange place to live. People can return to Morocco whenever they want if they're Moroccan, but of course, everyone wants to go to Spain. This place fills up quickly, so no one can stay forever. People are issued identification cards with expiration dates, usually three months at most. You can reregister if you like, but that doesn't mean you'll be given another card. If the authorities find you without a card, out you go. Of course, people try to stay in the CETI as long as possible, and if they can't, they live on the streets until they are picked up by the police."

I asked him how long he had been here. He taps his fingers as he counts, managing to fill one hand and begin on another. "Six months," he said at last. "So I am one of the elders here. It's the most senior-level position I have ever worked." Omar laughed at his own joke, but before I could press more questions on him, he stopped. Before us was the green entrance gate with people idling just beyond. The stout Spanish patrol officers who ensured that no one passed without authorization were smoking cigarettes, just like Omar, whose cigarette was now down to a nub.

"This is the way in and out," said Omar. "It closes at midnight and those people outside of it will remain there until the next day."

Omar explained how, nearly every day since his arrival, he had attempted to board a boat bound for Spain, many of them filled with refugees. He avoided the asylum office, which would have revoked his entry permit, and otherwise went to the dock looking for a way to slip onboard a ship without being noticed. "I have met many, many others who have gone across the sea, to a better life," he said, "perhaps that hope rubbed off on me. But others . . ."

In 2017, more than three thousand migrants passed through the Melillan CETI, residing here on average for three months or less, causing the facility to constantly overfill its estimated capacity of five hundred people. At one point in 2015, at the height of the so-called migration crisis, there were more than two thousand people who called this CETI home at the same time. Those who had gone through the gate and had been cleared for temporary residence here were the lucky ones. Jumping the fence was the only other way in, and to do so and not end up with bloodied hands and torn clothes from the barbed wire was the least of your worries. If a border guard found a migrant before anyone else, he was not required to check age or medical needs. Instead, he would turn the migrant around and send the person back to the other side of the fence. Others, including the many migrants that are processed for deportation for various reasons are sent to *Centros de Internamiento de Extranjeros*, or CIE, deportation centers that are run on the Spanish mainland.

It is one of the great ironies for migrants attempting to get to Spain through Melilla or Ceuta without asylum. They are put on a boat or plane and are sent north to the mainland, where they have tried to get for weeks or months or even years, only to be sent right back to their countries of origin soon thereafter. While they are arguably given better living conditions than many have likely had since their journey began—Spanish law requires that CIEs must not be prisonlike in nature or character—there are signs that the Spanish system is leaning toward the criminalization of migration that has become second nature in the United States. In late 2017, protests erupted in Andalusia when the Spanish government attempted to house overflow migrants in a prison that was under construction. Their solution had been simply to give the prison a more camp-like name, but that didn't fool anyone. The government did bow to pressure and in less than a month after the protests began, the migrants were transferred to an up-to-code facility elsewhere. But that's not likely to be the last time Spanish authorities will attempt something like this, and that may be why José, who was visibly shaken when I described the youth cages in the United States, kept abreast of developments that hinted at much harsher times to come for migrants seeking refuge.

The Melilla airport was only a couple miles from the CETI, and I still had some hours to fill before my early evening flight, so I said my goodbyes to Omar, giving him the entire pack of smokes and the lighter before heading off by foot along the crispy asphalt road that snaked along the border fence.

At the first bend in the road, on a small hill, I came upon a recently built mosque. There were dozens of cars parked on the street and people in full dress arriving for prayer. Outside the mosque, a graveyard flowed down the hillside toward the border fence, where the graveyard continued onto the other side, the dead unaware of which country they belong to—there is no citizenship in the afterlife. Not far from here, toward the downtown area of the city, there is another, much larger cemetery entirely on the Spanish side of Melilla. It was one of the first things I saw when I arrived in Melilla. This cemetery overlooks the sea, prime acreage that is surrounded by condos and a winding road. It is breathtaking. The cemetery's tombs are individual and coffin-shaped, and each of them lies on the cement surface of the cemetery, as if they are about to be buried or someone neglected to bury them all. Given that the cemetery looks out onto the Mediterranean Sea, where thousands of bodies go unburied each year, these tombs seem like an appropriate homage.

Compared to the U.S.–Mexican border bridge at Laredo, which felt almost like a bureaucratic afterthought, the Spanish–Moroccan border fence is the type of wall I imagined Trump had in mind. The three layers of the fence stand like soldiers in formation and, at least on the Spanish side, are in pristine condition. Though there were modern guard towers on the Spanish side, I spotted no occupants. The fence, so intimidating in the photos I had seen of it, was not being guarded. Then it hit me: no one was climbing this side of the fence to find refuge in Morocco.

So I decided to be the first, somewhat, and climbed halfway up the Spanish side to have a better look at the other side. The differences were immediately noticeable; while Spain had put up a fence, Morocco had built a barricade. On the fence farthest from where I hung, at around the same height, a coil of barbed wire hooped in a horizontal line. The wall was not the same model as the one I clung to, and the Moroccan guards had set it at an incline, adding inversion to an already difficult climb. Between Spain's simple fence and Morocco's advanced model, there was a third, much smaller fence in the middle, half as high as the other two, with heavy steel wires webbing toward the top of the main fences to reinforce them. Guards from either country could easily patrol the fence line from the tarmac paths that lay on the other side of this smaller fence. I jumped down quickly after a passing car honked at me, and continued my walk.

A mile or so later I spotted a whitewashed two-story barrack where, from a second-floor terrace, a shirtless Moroccan border guard with black, curly hair and a cigarette in his mouth was hanging his washed uniform to dry in the afternoon sunlight. He nodded to me, unconcerned, from the other side of the fence. I was startled at the casualness of his chore, just as I had been taken by the border guard at the Rio Grande who was able to recommend, in perfect Spanish, a good taco. It made me think of Francisco Cantú's book, *The Line Becomes a River*, a complicated yet poetic memoir of his time as a border agent and what it meant to forcefully prevent people from fulfilling their dire need to migrate. I realized that I was struggling with the humanity that comes in conflict with an occupation engendered by something I fundamentally disagreed with, the heartbeat of a hardline reality.

The border that I saw on this day, however, was difficult to reconcile with what I had read about in a *Guardian* article from 2010 in which José was interviewed by the writer Nick Davies as part of a bigger story regarding Melilla's border violations. As bad as José described the current situation, it was nothing compared to what Melilla had been like a decade before. Davies writes: "a man who had worked on the fence told me he would arrive at work in the morning to find his ladder covered in blood, where migrants had tried to use it to climb into the city and had become victims of the razor wire. Some made it over the fence. Some managed to smuggle themselves into the city in the backs of cars. Human Rights Watch found that children travelling alone were still finding their way in and were being held by the Spanish in an old fort, La Purisima, where they were beaten by staff, robbed and assaulted by older children, and kept in punishment cells for up to a week without bedding or toilets before being shoved back into Morocco where the police might give them another beating and put them out on to the streets to fend for themselves."

And even that was better than what had happened a few years prior, when dozens of migrant injuries and deaths had come at the hands of Spanish and Moroccan authorities. I wondered if those violent times had indeed passed into a nonviolent but aggressive stalemate, like that at the Korean border for instance, which has been patrolled by armed guards for nearly seventy years. The fence that day, however, was quiet and carried the eerie morbidity of the Wild West ghost towns near Reno. A few olive trees were growing across the road on which cars sped by from time to time. I looked back to see the guard adding a pair of pants to the line, apparently his only pair, as he had stripped to his underwear—a man of flesh and bone, destined to spend his life maintaining international segregations that wouldn't matter when it was his own turn to head toward the afterlife.

I arrived at the airport drenched in sweat, my black bag heavier, somehow, than when I started this walk three miles ago at the CETI. After I took a moment to rest, I continued toward passport control, where the customs officer informed me that my one-year visa had just expired. He handed it back to me and sure enough, the date stated I was four days over my visa term.

"I'm sorry," I said, "I am finishing up a fellowship at the University of Granada."

"So?"

"I'm here doing research," I stammered, before remembering the key to dealing with immigration officials, "but I'm leaving in a few days. I'm not staying."

The officer nodded robotically and told me to wait while he conferred with his supervisor. I watched them shrugging their shoulders in that distinctly Spanish manner and speaking half-heartedly, as the supervisor held my navy-blue passport in his hand. They acted exactly like the reality we were inhabiting: the airport was not a place of real concern for immigration here in Melilla and an American was far down on the list of people to detain or keep off a plane, though the soundness of that policy was questionable. I could hear others in line behind me growing restless—the two officers were the only ones on duty. Finally the supervisor came over.

"You are a researcher?" he asked.

"Yes," I replied. "But I'm leaving next week to go back to the U.S."

"Do you have a proof of a plane ticket?"

I pulled one up from my phone. He gave it a look, then shrugging his shoulders again, waved his hand toward his subordinate.

"Let him through."

It did not escape me that this privilege was something all of those living in the CETI would have died for.

———

My time in Spain had been fruitful and fraught. I had been fortunate for the opportunity to learn the immigration laws from an entirely different vantage point, both as a lawyer and a foreigner, and yet doing so meant that I was not in the United States when Trump escalated the war on immigrants to an unprecedented level. I know, however, that Alejandra enjoyed being back in Spain, near her family after five years away, all of whom were helping Chloe learn Spanish. Her family couldn't have been any kinder, always willing to make a phone call on my behalf, or take care of Chloe while Alejandra and I spent time together or made progress on our work. Such a need arose as we packed our bags, ready to return to the United States.

We had all been following the news for the past several days. The *Aquarius*, a ship overflowing with 630 refugees, had been denied entry in the ports of Italy, now under the control of the Five Star Movement and Minister of the Interior Matteo Salvini who tweeted "Close the Doors" as it lay in Mediterranean waters, and Malta. Spain, also led by a new government following the replacement of conservative Mariano Rajoy with socialist Pedro Sánchez, offered to accept the ship and the migrants in the port of Valencia. The migrant lives were completely at the whim of European politics, denied entry into one country where a short time ago they would have been accepted, and accepted in a country where they would've likely been denied before. In Italy and many countries, direct or indirect culpability for refugee deaths is no longer political suicide, but instead has become an applaudable uncompromising approach.

While the offer was an inspiring rebuke to the anti-migration wave—"Fortress Europe"—spreading through Europe, the logistics were complicated. At first, the ship floated between Italian and Maltese islands for two days, until the Spanish government stepped up. Italy, perhaps remorseful, offered two ships to assist the overcrowded *Aquarius*. Thus began a four-day journey to Valencia, hampered by bad weather and perilous conditions, while the refugees endured, already several days into a journey that began on clandestine boats that left from the coast of Libya. The ships, accustomed to much smaller cargo and built for short-term stays on board, were unprepared for such an extended journey and tempers ran high among the uncomfortable and frustrated refugees and crew. Many of the refugees had been rescued from the sea and some had to be resuscitated after swallowing significant amounts of seawater. While grateful for Spain's willingness to accept the ships and the refugees, the officials and refugees on board all would have preferred docking at the closest port.

By Saturday night, it had become clear that the long journey would be coming to a successful end on the morning of the fifth day. Alejandra and I made plans with her parents to take care of Chloe on Sunday morning. Alejandra's father let us borrow his car, and, at five thirty in the morning, Alejandra and I were parking near Valencia's port area. I was glad to have Alejandra along; she had offered unconditional support while I was at Karnes and JFK and other places I went when we didn't have help with Chloe, but she was an activist in her own right, and her presence, as it always did, inspired me.

Valencia, where Alejandra was born, is Spain's shipping capital and the busiest commercial port in the Mediterranean. It is home to the world-famous architect Santiago Calatrava, and because of this the city center abounds in swooping, avian architecture. Yet the port itself isn't particularly remarkable—cranes, containers, and merchant vessels all crowd for space. While the port is used as a recreational space for the city, Valencia is hundreds of miles from the Strait of Gibraltar and only recently, with the oversaturation of nearby Barcelona, has it become a destination for travelers other than those heading to the Balearic Islands, or the occasional cruise ship calling to port in its marina.

We arrived to find dozens of private sailboats tethered to the dock and the remnants of an outdoor concert held the night before. The ground was cluttered with beer cans, plastic cocktail cups, and memories of a good time. Workers slowly separated the metal bars that made up the stage, folded up the tents promising Desperados to a thirsty crowd, and other men in bright orange jumpsuits swept up the trash that littered the sidewalk and the streets. Alejandra asked a nearby worker what concert had just been held and he replied, "Fito & Fitipaldis," a duo that was Spain's answer to the Goo Goo Dolls and remained, despite their 1990s alt-rock sound, enormously popular. I had no idea who they were, but Alejandra began singing the lyrics to their most famous song, "*Soldadito marinero.*" Though the song is about unrequited love, its title, translated to "Little Soldier of the Sea," was a fitting description of the three ships and refugees soon to arrive.

Alejandra drove on until we arrived at the cruise ship dock. As she parked, I tried not to think again of the word "shipping" as it is used by U.S. border guards to refer to deported immigrants. At the entrance, however, were six police officers that refused to let us through.

"No one without authorization can enter," one of them told me.

"And where can we receive this authorization?"

But the officer shook his head and refused to tell me. I debated with him, engaging in one of Spain's national pastimes, and while we went back and forth and I pulled out every credential I was carrying, he would not let me through. More officers joined in the debate, looking over my papers, asking questions about my reasons for being here. I exaggerated and indulged in elaborate explanations, as I knew Spaniards appreciated this. Alejandra turned off the engine, stepped out of the car and joined in, doing her best to negotiate our entrance. The officer I first spoke with briefly walked away, gripping his walky-talky in front of his mouth in a way that prevented me from lip-reading what he was saying. I whispered to Alejandra, "In the U.S., we would have been arrested by now."

While we waited, I asked the officers if they'd watched Spain's disappointing opening match with Portugal in the World Cup on Friday night. "Fucking Cristiano Ronaldo," quipped one officer, referring to Portugal's star who had scored all three of his team's goals, resulting in the tie with Spain. Many teams, and some of the best teams, competing in the World Cup are comprised nearly entirely of immigrants or first-generation naturalized citizens so that the words "France" or "Morocco" across their jerseys reflect a two-tiered system: acceptance in the sports world that has yet to translate to the real world. When France won the World Cup a month later, comedian Trevor Noah jokingly congratulated Africa for winning the World Cup.

The officer returned from his brief conversation on the walky-talky. I thought he'd tell us to get lost, but instead he offered directions. "You need to go to the Swiss headquarters," he said jerking his thumb behind him. "The migrants are to be sent there later today, and people from various organizations are waiting there to greet them. But I can't guarantee that they'll let you in there either."

The Swiss headquarters, as Alejandra explained to me, was where the Swiss sailing team had set up its operations during the 32nd Annual America's Cup, a sailing competition, held in Valencia. The building had kept this moniker with the Valencians, though the Cup competition had long since concluded and moved to other locations. It was a warehouse-style building immediately next door to the Port of Americas, a vast, modern, multitiered cultural and administrative center located in the marina. Valencia had hosted the event in 2007, going as far as building this entire submarina to accommodate it. The Port of Americas building was its centerpiece, with terraces to lounge with drinks from nearby overpriced restaurants. Like the leftovers from the concert near the point of arrival of the three migrant-laden ships, the migrants would be processed at the convergence of Spanish wealth. There was a distressing duality in contemplating the swanky seafaring competition once housed here and the survival mission—which included pregnant women and parentless children—now arriving.

The facility that had been set aside for the migrants was a large, high-ceilinged area. We arrived to find it already buzzing with activity: government and nonprofit aid workers were everywhere. It reminded me of the gathering of volunteer lawyers at JFK during the travel ban. If I couldn't be in the United States while the zero-tolerance policy was in effect, I could at least volunteer here. Part of my research had been to study EU and Spanish immigration law and policy. What I discovered was a system vastly different from ours, yet no less problematic. While Europe took in more asylum-seeking immigrants than the United States, many of them were confined to campgrounds or ad hoc villages that everyone could move freely within, yet were restricted in their ability to leave, and lacked many basic necessities. There was also the Dublin Regulations, which dictated that refugees arriving into the EU by law had to apply for asylum in the country where they first landed. Germany, which has no ocean border and is protected from migrant ships by its southern neighbors like a quarterback with an offensive line, was the strongest proponent of the regulations. This is depicted by German journalist Wolfgang Bauer in his book, *Crossing the Sea: With Syrians on the Exodus to Europe.* Bauer finds that most refugees don't carry their documentation with them when they cross and use fake names upon arrival, avoiding at all costs EURODAC, the EU's fingerprint database of asylum seekers over fourteen. That way, they can keep moving until they have arrived in a northern European country with lower rates of unemployment and apply for asylum there, thus outwitting the Dublin Regulations.

After our arrival I went to check-in, though I had not formally signed up to volunteer. I was one of four thousand people who had called or sent an email to the overwhelmed local Valencian government, and never received a response. A young woman directed me to the volunteer coordinator of the Spanish Red Cross, who informed me that my services were not needed.

"You don't need the help of an immigration lawyer?" I asked. "I speak both English and Spanish."

"Do you speak Arabic or French?" the coordinator asked.

I shook my head, wincing a bit at the acknowledgment. It was a limitation that had slowed my research and made impossible many interactions with migrants while I was in Spain.

"Did you get fingerprinted and have a background check?"

I shook my head again.

"Then you can't volunteer today, I'm sorry."

I gathered from the order of her questions that if I spoke Arabic or French she would have overlooked the fingerprints and background check, since they had sufficient volunteers but hardly any with that language capability. It was heartening, nonetheless, to see the two thousand volunteers outnumber the arriving migrants more than three to one, and the government support, both at the federal level in Madrid and here locally in Valencia.

Alejandra seeing my rejection, asked what I wanted to do next. "Whatever you want," she said encouragingly, "if you want to stay here, I will stay with you."

I took in our surroundings and said, "Let's stay."

In truth, I was starving to see solidarity, to watch as men and women who had never met, accept each other into their lives with compassion. I needed to see strangers not divided by fear, but united in humanity, in breathing the same air, sharing the same space, European, African, born here or just arriving, intertwined in something bigger and more important than politics. In seeing this, I hoped that it would minimize the aching, the embarrassment, the outright hostility I had been feeling in seeing my own country separate parents from their children at the border. At the same time, it was complicated and problematic for me to see the frenzy surrounding what should be a simple arrival, an offer of safe harbor. Supporters could not separate this event from their politics, and I was as guilty as those standing nearby with signs, including an Italian student who held a sign that read: REFUGEES, SORRY FOR SALVINI. I wondered aloud to Alejandra if humanity had become politicized. We watched as reporters filled the first floor of the Port of Americas building, where tables had been set up for their computers; coffee and breakfast was provided for them on another table against the wall. The suffering and survival of *the other*, undergirded and inseparable from the policies and reactions of the First World, were becoming front-page news.

Still, we stayed, and no one seemed to mind that Alejandra and I watched the scene unfold as we held hands. A group of medical volunteers had left to meet the refugees now coming off the boat, and in the distance I could vaguely make out their vehicle returning with busloads of people in tow. There was some commotion and more volunteers from the facility ran out to the entrance ready to greet the refugees. Alejandra and I watched as the motorcade drove straight up to the curb closest to the doors and stood aside to let volunteers guide migrants from the buses to the reception center entrance. Translators in pink vests transmitted the queries of the medical professionals. I heard one engage a migrant who responded to English by saying that he is from the Gambia, where, I later learned, English was the official language. *Are you sick?* asked the translator. *Are you in pain? Do you need food? Water? Let me help you walk.* The Gambian man was handed a blanket and a bottle of water and ushered through the vast door, underneath a sign that said WELCOME HOME in five different languages. The phrase was meant to offer a feeling of arriving to a promising new life. The moment of arrival was undeniably beautiful and uplifting, almost unrealistically so. Such a moment had been missing from the United States for years, where refugee arrivals were uniformly met with criminal suspicion or surreptitious government maneuvering. After witnessing such a promising procession, I hugged Alejandra. When our eyes met, I could see her steely green eyes had filled with tears. We had seen some things together, and as a psychologist she had worked with immigrant families and knew the struggles, but something about returning to her hometown and seeing how everyone was reacting overwhelmed her.

We were silent on the drive back to Alejandra's parents' house, both of us preferring to be alone with our thoughts. They had lifted me to great hope, a feeling that was dampened later when the Spanish government acknowledged that not all of those arriving on the boat would be able to stay in the country; some will be sent back, having failed to qualify for asylum or other forms of immigration relief. The WELCOME HOME sign we had seen felt like false advertising. And yet there would undoubtedly be more boats, there would undoubtedly be pressure from the conservative parties to tighten Spain's immigration laws, there would be neighboring nations more than happy to shove off its own migrant issues onto Spanish shoulders. The dueling national policies within the fractured European Union seem to be fighting to the death, though it is not their own blood that is being spilled. In the United States, it would be like Texas, New Mexico, Arizona, and California all having different border policies, one denying refugees while another accepts them, one neutral, one positively swept up into anti-immigrant hysteria. For now, Spain remains the most recent recipient of this hot potato system, but for how long this would be the case would be anyone's guess. With more countries slipping politically toward the right, things would likely worsen. I would never stop hoping, however, that the kindness I saw in Valencia could also one day become the global norm.

Back in the United States, the complicated work of reuniting families was proving to be as difficult as it was to prevent them from being separated in the first place. The Trump administration, like a spoiled kid who wants his parents to clean up after him, suggested to the federal court judge in San Diego who issued the order to reunite families that the ACLU and other nonprofit organizations should be in charge of reuniting the families. I had read accounts of children being put on planes and sent across the country to orphanage-like facilities and stories of parents recounting how, even after reunification, the children had ceased to recognize them or blamed them for abandoning them. One father would never be reunited with his child because he had committed suicide after his child was taken from him.

As the government finally began its attempt to comply with the judicial order to reunify children with their parents, it became clear that the right hand had little idea what the left hand was doing. In district court in the District of Columbia, colleagues spoke about the government promising not to deport two plaintiffs in their lawsuit before a Friday hearing, and then finding out during the hearing that they were both already on a plane back to El Salvador. They said the government attorney in court that day was also shocked, and it was obvious that he knew nothing about the deportation. The judge ordered them both returned and threatened to hold Jeff Sessions in contempt.

There is a photo that I have returned to often during the days that the United States continued and even expanded its family separation policy. The photo, by John Moore, shows a two-year-old in a pink jacket, mouth wide, frozen amid a deep cry. She is facing her mother, hoping for comfort, but her mother's hands are placed firmly against a white U.S. border patrol vehicle, while a border patrol officer in plastic gloves stands behind the mother, searching her. The caption reads: "A two-year-old Honduran asylum seeker cries as her mother is searched and detained near the U.S.–Mexico border."

Though there was an outcry among Trump supporters that this photo was nothing more than fake news, and while it was later discovered that the child and mother were not separated, the power of the image and the evil of the policy, coupled with widespread domestic and international condemnation, led Trump to sign an executive order ending family separation on June 20, 2018, just days before Alejandra, Chloe, and I boarded a plane for the United States. The executive order was the policy equivalent of using paper towels to clean up the Exxon oil spill, was less of a compromise and more of a contravention to the 1997 *Flores* settlement, which barred the detention of minors for more than twenty days in secure and unlicensed facilities. It was as if Trump thought he were making a deal by saying, *Fine, we will no longer separate parents from their children, but then we must be allowed to keep families detained for as long as we want*. The Obama administration had tried to make a similar argument in 2015, telling a federal district court judge that the *Flores* settlement should only apply to unaccompanied minors and not minors arriving with their parents. The district court judge disagreed, but as I saw during my time along the border and continuing on to the present, the judge's ruling has never been fully implemented or respected. In the aftermath of the policy, parents were forced into a Faustian bargain: waive the *Flores* protections their children have, thus causing the children to remain detained with them indefinitely, or consent to the children going into the Office of Refugee Resettlement (ORR) custody without them and being protected by the *Flores* Settlement Agreement. It didn't make this decision any easier that there was no mention of reuniting families or a plan for such action; the Trump administration had left that issue for other institutions and government departments to deal with.

And now an unfathomable amount of psychological damage has since been done to so many families. The likelihood for many of these younger immigrant children—some of tender age, barely able to walk and still breastfeeding—was that that they would not be reunited with their parents, not anytime soon, maybe not ever. Many children, like Chloe, do not even know their parents' names—they are simply *Mama* or *Papa*. And now they are gone, sent to somewhere in the Northern Triangle. There wasn't an official or recognized process for reuniting families, for helping families cope with the psychological trauma inflicted upon them. The Trump administration had created a mess and no one knew how to clean it up.

PART VI

THE END OF THE BEGINNING

. . . .

The suspense: the fearful, acute suspense: of standing idly by while the life of one we dearly love, is trembling in the balance; the racking thoughts that crowd upon the mind, and make the heart beat violently, and the breath come thick, by the force of the images they conjure up before it; the desperate anxiety *to be doing something* to relieve the pain, or lessen the danger, which we have no power to alleviate; the sinking of soul and spirit, which the sad remembrance of our helplessness produces; what tortures can equal these; what reflections of endeavours can, in the full tide and fever of the time, allay them!

—*Charles Dickens*, Oliver Twist

Chloe's eyelids cracked gently open, revealing the light-blue irises.

"We're here, Chloe. It's time to wake up," Alejandra said gently.

She rubbed her eyes with two small fists and stretched out, her feet dipping into the aisle of the airplane. Her legs were in my lap and her upper body on Alejandra's. Nothing tests a child's maturity, or a parent's patience, more than how she acts on long plane rides. Our flight from Valencia to Sacramento took a full day and included a layover in Dallas, which only delayed the length of the trip. Chloe, however, behaved like a young adult, albeit one excited for an adventure. Though she got bored with her toys and the films we encouraged her to watch, though she wanted to wander the aisles and stare up at passengers by way of introduction, Chloe didn't shed a tear. She also didn't sleep, not until the very end of the flight, which meant that we also didn't sleep. But at least during the first leg of the trip, every member of our family felt ready for our next big life step. I had accepted a position at UC Davis School of Law in their Immigration Law Clinic, one of the first of its kind in the nation. By taking on complex cases, ones that often lie at the intersection between immigration and criminal law, the clinic served to set precedents for future cases across the country. Due to its proximity to the Central Valley, the clinic works with a variety of documented and undocumented immigrants, and many farmworkers. Importantly, it is also co-counsel on the *Flores* Settlement Agreement, meaning I would get firsthand experience in the ongoing and contentious litigation surrounding the Agreement and its applications. Because the clinic was under the direction of two legendary immigration lawyers, to say that I was incredibly fortunate to be there would have been an understatement. I had also come full circle: the Immigration Law Clinic where I would be working was the very same one that had inspired me and taught me so much as a law student.

But in Dallas, as Chloe and Alejandra chowed down on fried chicken, ribs, and cornbread, the reality of the America we were coming back to set in. If that had only meant Alejandra giving Chloe English lessons—*fork, napkin, table, chair*—I would have found the experience charming. Instead, I marveled at the ubiquity of "Make America Great Again" hats and "patriot" T-shirts, as if what it meant to love this country had been branded by a guy who loved to stamp his name on things. And without missing a beat, his name flashed on a nearby TV screen. "Supreme Court Upholds Trump Travel Ban." The screen momentarily changed to show President Trump's capitalized tweets. Even he seemed to be surprised at the Supreme Court's 5–4 decision "SUPREME COURT UPHOLDS TRUMP TRAVEL BAN. Wow!" Neil Gorsuch, the justice sitting in Merrick Garland's seat, had cast the decisive vote for the majority, which found that the travel ban was not discriminatory because the word "Muslim" never appears once in the language of the ban. When the news anchor briefly quoted from Justice Sotomayor's written dissent, I immediately googled it to read. With searing and impassioned detail and language, she spoke to every frustration I had.

> Taking all the relevant evidence together, a reasonable observer would conclude that the Proclamation was driven primarily by anti-Muslim animus, rather than by the Government's asserted national-security justifications. Even before being sworn into office, then-candidate Trump stated that "Islam hates us," warned that "we're having problems with the Muslims, and we're having problems with Muslims coming into the country," promised to enact a "total and complete shut down of Muslims entering the United States," and instructed one of his advisers to find a "legal" way to enact a Muslim ban. The President continued to make similar statements well after his inauguration . . . despite several opportunities to do so, President Trump has never disavowed any of his prior statements about Islam.

Justice Sotomayor didn't just point out the obvious, but used court cases to support the dissent, including pointing out the court's hypocrisy in a recent case, *Masterpiece Cakeshop v. Colorado Civil Rights Commission*, where a baker refused to bake a cake for a same-sex couple's wedding celebration, which was decided based almost entirely on disparaging comments that the commission made about the cake shop owner's religious beliefs. Expanding her outrage, Sotomayor also cited *Korematsu v. U.S.*, a 1944 Supreme Court decision that upheld the Executive Order sending all Japanese into internment camps, regardless of whether they were U.S. citizens or not:

By blindly accepting the Government's misguided invitation to sanction a discriminatory policy motivated by animosity toward a disfavored group, all in the name of a superficial claim of national security, the Court redeploys the same dangerous logic underlying *Korematsu* and merely replaces one "gravely wrong" decision with another.

Nearly all Supreme Court dissents end with "I respectfully dissent." Sotomayor, I noticed, had left off "respectfully." It was a small snub to an otherwise overwhelming truth, one that I was now feeling the irony of: we had arrived in the United States on the exact date that nationals from Syria, Libya, Iran, Yemen, Chad, Somalia, North Korea, and Venezuela would no longer be able to do so.

My mind returned briefly back to Spain and how I had asked *What comes next?* when refugees had stepped onto Spanish soil in Valencia, contemplating the policy decisions that would follow. Immediately upon arriving in the United States, I grasped that the same question was an exercise in contemplating our worst fears. Among other sweeping changes, the Trump administration has, in a short amount of time, just while we were in Spain, canceled Temporary Protected Status for nationals of several countries, leaving hundreds of thousands without legal status; attempted to end the Deferred Action for Childhood Arrivals program, leaving those who were brought here as young children to fight in the final moments of a roller-coaster ride they have been on for close to two decades; and removed twenty years of case law that allowed survivors of domestic violence to apply for asylum with the nonchalant and inexplicable swipe of a pen. The question is not a philosophical debate between equally plausible alternatives in the United States, but a terrifying Pandora's box that now includes tent cities in the scorching Texas desert and mounting suggestions of gutting due process completely for all immigrants arriving to and already living in the United States.

An announcement came on the airport speaker system and broke my reverie. Alejandra tapped my shoulder. "They are boarding for our flight," she said. We gathered our things and I picked Chloe up into my arms. For once, I looked forward to the doldrums of flying, for I knew that the moment we landed in California, I would be hitting the ground running.

———

Don't read your email," warned Holly. "It's . . . I don't even know what to say."

We were on a train speeding south. Holly was one of my new bosses, a fierce advocate with so much experience that I often jotted down comments she would toss off. We were on our way to Los Angeles, to appear in federal district court as part of a team of lawyers challenging the federal government's treatment of immigrant youth in detention centers. Outside the window, glimpses of the Pacific Ocean flashed by, at times filling the glass entirely like a dark-blue premonition. Near Oxnard, we cut inland and into agricultural fields with neat, green rows. Farmworkers with bandanas or wide brimmed hats, blue jeans, and sweat-dampened long-sleeved shirts were hunched over or walking among the rows. The train had slowed down near a group of laborers squatting in a semicircle in the middle of a strawberry field. The scene was so familiar to me that I could imagine their Spanish or indigenous language chatter, bits of earth spread through their fingers and permanently pressed beneath their fingernails and into their calloused palms. They ate tortillas stuffed with *carnitas*. It was an almost serene lunch.

"Alvaro" was all that was written in the subject line. The sender was another lawyer we worked with, and the name was of a seventeen-year-old boy, detained for several months. "I've just been informed that Alvaro attempted suicide this morning. He is no longer in the detention center but in a nearby hospital. Fwding the address to you." Alvaro's only crime and the entire reason for his detention was that he is an immigrant, which, undoubtedly, in this country and at this moment, is one of the more severely punished crimes. The immigrants currently held in detention centers and jails across the United States are criminalized for their very existence, and thus, for Alvaro and others, their only liberty lies in no longer existing.

These are not the separated children and parents that appear on the news. This is another, vaster population, separated from their families as well, but not at the direct urging of Jeff Sessions and Donald Trump. This is a stable and constant tragedy, with years behind it and years ahead of it. While around three thousand children were separated from their parents during the "zero-tolerance" policy, there are five or six times as many unaccompanied minors in detention at any one time in the United States. Eighty percent of children who arrive in the United States come alone. More than one-fourth of the entire detained immigrant population, which was close to forty thousand in 2018, is under eighteen.

I had visited Alvaro less than a week ago, on a Thursday morning. It was the third time that I had met with him at the detention center. On the first visit, I remember that he was energetic and charismatic, and he convinced me that the half dozen slices on his forearm were only to get the guards' attention. The guards at the detention center soon after gave him a bloody ear from repeatedly slamming him to the concrete floor, or that's what he told me over the phone at least. The blood was dried and crusted on his right earlobe when I visited him the second time. By the third visit, his energy was tapering off, but his indomitable spirit continued to rankle the guards. The guards begin to cut his already limited privileges and jump at any excuse to punish him, especially with violence. He looked for ways to show them that they were not winning and that he would survive. The punishments become worse.

He said something to me on the last visit, which I wrote down on the first page of my yellow legal pad so that I see it every day I use the notepad to take down the stories of immigrant youth like him. I pulled the notepad out of my bag. The words are scribbled in blue and they shake with the train and my hands. *Me gusta America, pero no me gusta lo que me hace.* I like America, but I don't like what it does to me.

It is a succinct description of immigrant detention in the United States. Apart from Alvaro, two other detained immigrant youths had recently expressed suicidal ideations to me, their past traumas combining with their current ones. One young man had a broken leg that randomly dislocated at the knee while he walked, but he was only given a brace that was a glorified sock; anything stronger would have come with metal screws and been dangerous and against the rules, according to those we spoke with. Another young man had a bullet lodged in his shoulder and a wrist that was shattered by a baseball bat in El Salvador and never properly set. We pushed the supervisors to get him x-rays, but nothing came of them. All of these youths just want to sleep at night, to close their eyes on this waking nightmare, and so they ask for sleeping medication, which, of course, they don't get. Instead, they are administered different variations of drug cocktails that keep them in a mental straight-jacket so that they behave. They are mostly listless, some nearly catatonic during the day.

The point of this treatment is to neuter an angry population, but the effect is the opposite. After suffering intense traumas, immigrant youth are retraumatized or further traumatized by abusive guards, conniving psychiatrists, and eternal detention. Unlike prisoners sentenced to prison for crimes, who know the length of their sentences and can "do their time," as the saying goes, because they know when the end is coming, these immigrant youths do not. They have been told they will be released next week and that was six months ago. They have been told they will be flown to a detention center in North Carolina, close to their father so he can visit, and then they are flown here, to California. They have been told to take these pills to help you feel happy, take these other ones to help you remain calm, and then they become someone else. They are confused. They feel betrayed. They become anxious. They become angry. They act out. Then their detention is prolonged because they are "dangerous"—it is a vicious cycle that can and has ended in suicide. There is no de-escalation. Instead, the federal government has a policy where children are "stepped up" to more secure facilities when they act out, often in direct response to triggering violence by guards, inappropriate medication for misdiagnosed conditions, or sheer helplessness. As they are "stepped up," their lives become more restricted, their hope thinner. Some youth I've spoken with are outside of their cells only seven or eight hours a day. As one youth told me, "I've been in America for four months and all I've done is suffer. A friend of mine in the next cell over asked to be deported, even though he's in the process of applying for asylum. I might do the same soon." That is why I was not surprised to receive the email regarding Alvaro, though it did not lessen the pain.

At the same time, something strange had begun to happen at home as well. My visits to Alvaro and other kids in the center started when I was only a week or two into my new position, but around that same time Chloe had begun to suffer night terrors. Unlike nightmares which are vivid and often memorable, a night terror was a very physical occurrence in which Chloe would thrash her sheets and converse out loud to herself. We could not touch her, as that would make it worse, and we were instructed never to try to wake her. Yet when she woke the next morning after a night terror, Chloe would not remember at all what had happened. After my third visit to the juvenile detention center, Chloe had a particularly passionate night terror in which she screamed with uncontrollable violence. The noise sliced into the quiet night like a machete cutting a marshmallow. I had not—and still have not—learned to deal with what goes on in the detention centers, but Chloe seemed to have connected to the intense experiences I was having during my visits. It was like a form of empathy, the scream I had long wanted to let out, when these kids recounted their stories of abuse and thoughts of suicide. Or it was the scream I heard beneath each word that the youth spoke, a soundtrack to overlay the scenes they depicted. On that night, as we tried anything to calm our daughter down, I looked at Alejandra, telling her gently that all was okay. I listened to her as well, letting her words soothe my feeling of helplessness.

———

The last cracks of a bloodred sun seep through the redwoods and pines. The sky is ash gray. The smoke from not-so-distant fires up and down California fills my nostrils. It looks and smells like the end of the world. Chloe's shouts of joy are carried in the air. I look from my seat on the wooden bench toward the green slide that she has just ridden down. As soon as her feet touch the ground, she runs toward the stairs again, ready to slide for the dozenth time. The park is small but hidden deep in a neighborhood at the edge of town, bordering the agricultural fields, such that we are often the only ones here in the evenings. Since it is next door to our house, it is like having our own park, an Eden away from it all.

This is our escape, or mine at least. For Chloe, it is our latest routine: moving three times in four years—each move transcontinental—has left her grasping for stability. For me, this is where I go to find perspective, to rediscover innocence. The simple act of enjoying a simple act is not so simple. Some days I struggle to grasp at joy, even in watching my daughter on the swing set, her hair flapping back and forth as she conquers her nascent fear of speed. She is my ground, whenever I lose myself to ruminating upon the devastating images and traumatic stories that I endlessly take in from immigrants. I don't want to start helping them, I just want to feel something uncomplicated . . .

This has been the upside to working at the clinic—seeing how supported our cause is by the nation at large. The good is mounting: a gay rabbi in Minnesota raised $5,000 in a week to help us reunite a young woman in detention with her older sister who did not have a home. When I first spoke on the phone with him, he told me "I want to help" and repeated it. When I asked him why, he said "My in-laws were Jews that arrived on a boat fleeing Nazi Germany and someone had to have helped them," as if that history were enough to explain his selfless gesture today. The next day, he bought a bed with his own money, and delivered it to the sister's new apartment so they no longer sleep on the floor.

Then the bigger victories arrive. An Asian American judge,

the daughter of Cantonese immigrants, issues an order protecting detained immigrant youth, like Alvaro, from harsh mistreatment, including the administration of psychotropic drugs without consent or oversight, prolonged detention, unprompted physical altercations, and the withholding of water, which had become a popular form of punishment. The same lawyer who litigated the original *Flores* settlement thirty years ago argues this case as well. I watch him at the podium, a silver-haired man, the leader of our team of lawyers, and the years suddenly peel away as he transforms with righteous indignation. The powerful federal government did not stand a chance. That it is a triumph also shows the moral abyss we have fallen into, when the issuance of a judicial precedent in the United States includes language ordering the federal government to no longer withhold water from detained immigrant youth.

Unimaginable events like these, like the zero-tolerance policy and its mass separation of parents and children, have ignited people to care now in many ways that only two years before would have been a fantasy. A small group of concerned citizens in a city near the detention center donated hundreds of dollars for the express purpose of having pizza delivered to the detained immigrant youth. Many of these youths have had to eat the same baloney sandwich with limp vegetables as their only meal day after day. Even in dire poverty, these Central American youths were raised on fresh food and know the difference between a week-old broccoli stalk and one freshly picked. That any of them would have thought they would get pizza in a place like this would have been cruel to suggest. Yet as I watch the six large pepperoni pizzas go behind the heavy steel door to Pod B on the first day, the smell of melted cheese and pepperoni lingering behind, I imagined hearing for the first time in the facility the sounds of boys laughing. Sometimes a simple act of compassion is the most powerful form of resistance there can be. This is the way back, this is how we actually make America great again.

At that moment, Chloe runs from a slide and over to the bench where I'm sitting, interrupting my thoughts with a surprise hug.

"*¿Vamos a casa?*" I ask her.

"*Una vez más, Papa, porfa.*"

"Okay."

She leaves a mention of innocence on my shoulder where she had lain her head while asking for more time to play. Every day working with immigrant youth, innocence is what I hope to help them find again. They have lost it somewhere in the desert on the way here or long before then. It is so easily lost and corrupted, and I hope Chloe can carry it to the precipice of adulthood without worry. And I hope that every immigrant youth can regain some of it, through pizza, through love, through the good that I have seen among us. Perhaps the United States can as well.

Chloe rushes back to the slide, ready for her last trip down before we go back to the house, where her mother is waiting for us. There is more responsibility now: our second daughter is on the way and will be born into this new world, whereas Chloe was already growing familiar with it. Still, they are among the lucky ones, even if neither of them knows it yet. Chloe laughs triumphantly as she exits the slide. I walk over to her. She holds my hand as we walk down the path. Pine needles scatter with a brief wind. A warm light emanates from our home. Through the window I can see Alejandra holding her belly that carries our unborn daughter. The sun has set, but it is not dark yet.

ACKNOWLEDGMENTS

I still don't quite believe that I have written a book or that it has been published, but if you are reading this, it must be true. And if it is true, it is only because of the following people and organizations:

The people I have had the honor to work with as their attorney—you are not an alien, you are not illegal. You are strong beyond words and wherever you may be, I am with you.

The Watsonville Law Center, especially Henry and Adriana, for the first and hardest lessons in advocating for immigrants through the legal system.

The staff, interns, members, and everyone at Atlas:DIY who welcomed me into their wonderful organization and taught me to believe in the future. Especially Becky McBride, whose sense of humor was essential in the foxhole.

My colleagues in the Immigrant Justice Corps fellowship, who I was lucky enough to be among for two years. Matt, Sussan, Nabila, Laura, and Kristen in particular, since they made me a better advocate and person through their friendship.

The Fulbright Program, the Fulbright Commission of Spain, and the University of Granada's Migration Institute, for the opportunity to start this book, see the issue of migration more globally and visit Melilla, an impactful trip if ever there was one. Plus, as a bonus, I met Jesus, Dillon, Casey, and Mary Clare who helped me along, one Nordés at a time.

Holly Cooper and Amagda Pérez, mentors since law school, friends and sheroes who I have the privilege of working with currently. And Leticia Saucedo, an early and constant support.

My editor, Michael Barron, who discovered my manuscript deep in the slush pile and managed to find a narrative that I didn't know it had and a voice that I didn't know I had. That manuscript became this book because of him and his singular efforts on a topic near to his heart.

Mis tíos Pia Barros and Jorge Montealegre, Bruja and Leon, and *Tío Memo* for helping me discover Chile on my own and for the early teachings in art and life which came to the surface while writing this book.

To the memory of my godfather, Fast Freddie Velasquez, who wouldn't have read this book because he didn't read books, but he sure would have been proud. Thinking of that helped me finish it.

Mis suegros y cuñados and everyone in the Piquer and Martinez families in Valencia and Alicante that gave me time, space, support and *jamón* while I wrote, unclear if anything would ever come of this. Special thanks to Jose, both a brother and a best friend.

My parents, Emma and John, who set a multicultural, humane example in the way they engaged with the world and raised me with a love and patience that I am striving to reach with my own children.

Speaking of which—Chloe and Mya, someday I hope you will read this book and learn something about your father and the world you were born into. If you are proud, then it was all worth it.

The last words of the book go to Alejandra, who inspired its first words and everything else I do. Even when you weren't with me, you were with me every step of the way.

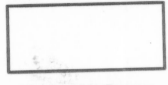